THE
MEMORY
CATCHER

WHEN ANGELS SPEAK, WHO WILL LISTEN?

BY SARAH HINZE
AND
LAURA HINZE LOFGREEN

Published by:
Vintage Bird Press and Three Orchard Productions

Printed in the United States of America

FORWARD

by Laura Hinze Lofgreen

There were perks growing up in a home with a mom who believed in angels. For instance, she offered a lot of prayer, prayer spoken like eloquent poems with beautiful language and heartfelt desire. We prayed when I needed to find my lost shoes or a report for school. We prayed when my little brother almost cut his finger off and had to go the hospital. We took turns saying prayers and gathered before bedtime each night, thanking God for the blessings of the day and asking for help where we struggled.

My mom, Sarah Hinze, speaks to God like He is in the room and there were times I felt He was. She knows God is real, not just a force pushing clouds through the sky, but a Father in Heaven who loves all His children and knows us by name. People she meets are treated with a respect and sincerity that is usually saved for close friends. No one is a stranger in her home. When her friends and acquaintances are troubled, my mom is one they can come to with trust. She seems to have a deep perspective on life that is unique. She believes with a simple but firm faith that we lived before in heaven and come to earth with a purpose when it is our time. She believes when we die our spirits return to heaven where we are judged and rewarded for our deeds on earth.

My mom mothered with reverence, always expressing gratitude that she was a mother. She told me the angels have a book of remembrance with golden pages and everything I do in love is recorded in heaven.

"One day you will sit with God and He will open the angel's book and you will remember all you did to honor Him," she said. The angels, whose presence Mom senses periodically, are generally of two types— unborn souls who are preparing to be born on earth, or deceased souls who have had their turn on earth and have returned to heaven. Mom's encounters with angels come through sensing their presence, spiritual dreams and sometimes actually hearing or seeing. The angels or heavenly beings might come with a message of encouragement, comfort, guidance, warning or protection. Difficult times in Mom's life are softened by the understanding that God loves her. She never doubts guardian angels are near.

Another benefit is my mom loves books. She still reads daily from scriptures, but her study does not stop there. She reads inspiring stories about people and uplifting spiritual experiences. Rather than skimming through pages of the latest tabloids, my mom might quote something from the Dead Sea Scrolls and the Nag Hammadi Texts.

My mom never spanked, grounded or put us children in "time out." Instead, she would sit us down and remind us, "Remember, we chose each other in heaven before we were born. We were best friends there and are now a family here on earth. You chose me to be your mother and I was honored. You loved your brothers and sisters so much you would never want to hurt them or be mean." It was a very convincing form of discipline.

My mom is not burdened by the typical cares of the world. Her wardrobe is modest and her home, although not immaculate, is always welcoming and comfortable.

For me, one of the best perks of growing up with a mom who believed in angels is she loved babies. She believes adamantly all souls have a right to birth. Being pregnant wasn't easy for her, but she welcomed it because she knew babies came from heaven. When she brought home a new little brother or sister from the hospital, wrapped in a blanket like a present from God, she knew her baby just days earlier had been an angel too.

She knows we all have angel potential within us if we remember who we really are . . . sad things can happen when we forget our true potential.

THE MEMORY CATCHER

My mom still believes in angels and she still loves babies. These two gifts have put her in an interesting position. From time to time she senses, and sometimes hears or sees, angel babies—spirits from heaven who desire their turn on earth. Because many unborn souls are being blocked or aborted when striving to come to earth, my mom feels their trauma and their pain. She has literally heard, and is greatly affected by, the crying of rejected unborn souls through the veil.

To help us better understand the needs of our unborn brothers and sisters, my mom has written six books in which she shares some of her encounters with unborn souls. Additionally, she has become a researcher, an interviewer—a "memory catcher" of the encounters of others with unborn souls who are eager to come to earth. I believe my mom, along with others, is called of God to do this work in behalf of unborn souls. Her work began small, but now my mom receives emails and phone calls from all over the world. Some share their encounters with unborn souls. Others report that, after reading one of my mom's books or hearing her speak, or contacting her personally, they decided not to abort a child and now they rejoice that the child has joined their family.

My mom is humble. She claims no personal expertise in her writings . . . the power is in the testimonies of those who have partaken in the divinity of the human spirit. These encounters strengthen our understanding of where we come from, why we need to come here and where we can go after this life.

Imagine spending hours upon hours with your own mother, listening as she shares the most meaningful experiences of her life. This has been my privilege. She has honored me by asking that I join her in writing about her life journey and the miracles associated with memories of angels and how these memories have saved lives. Here is her story.

PART I

HOMESICK FOR HEAVEN

To the East

Some might call it a game—the way I left my body, floated above myself and tried to leave the four walls of my house—but to me, trying to get back to heaven was not a game at all.

The first time I spontaneously left my body, I wasn't even sure what I was doing. My mom, Edna Garland Street, was in the kitchen snapping green beans we'd picked from the garden in the coolness of early morning. She rarely let me cook with her, so as she put a pot of water on to boil she said, "Go play now, Sarah."

I went into Mom's bedroom and sat at her dresser table. It was one of my favorite places to play. I loved the jewelry and the perfume. I loved to pat some powder on my face and dab on some bright red lipstick as I had seen her do. I stared into the mirror and somehow saw a different image of myself . . . *I'm not just a little girl, I'm much older.*

My earliest memories included God—that I had lived with Him and He cared for me. I seemed to innately "know" Him. Staring into the mirror, I reflected, *"Where are you, God? Why am I here in this place? Do my mom and dad know that I am really your child?"*

I could smell frying bacon and hear boiling water bubbling.

"I love my home here, but I really miss my heavenly home."

With that thought I slipped from my body and rose to the ceiling, looking down at my five–year-old self. I had a desire to keep going and head east, but the ceiling seemed to be as far as I had power to go. The real me, my floating self, knew if I could just push past the ceiling, I could return to God. Then suddenly I was back in my body.

Once I learned to leave my body, I repeated this scenario for several weeks. I would wander back to my spot at the vanity when Mom was busy, sometimes when I wanted to spend time with her, but she was occupied with other things.

When Mom or dad spent time with me, held me in their lap or read to me my favorite picture books, their love caused me to forget the cause of my sadness; I was homesick for heaven.

One day, when I was lonely for God again, I was sitting in front of my mom's vanity. I was out of my body and I saw myself from the back. I had a three dimensional view of my little girl self. I noticed how my hair curled down the back of my neck and how I sat ramrod straight on the vanity bench. In some ways, I hardly recognized me. I was wondering again how I could move past the ceiling to go home to God when a male voice thundered from the unseen world, "Sarah, get back into your body right now and don't you ever do that again!" It was a voice of great authority, like the voice of God!

Immediately I shot back into my body. As much as I yearned for the freedom of escaping my body, I never did so again for I knew I had to obey.

But I had learned something important. There was an unseen world around me where God and angels could see me and talk to me. . . I knew I was not alone. *(I share this personal story because I think other children may be having the same experiences, thus there is such an important need for children to be loved and cherished, as well as taught about God when they are very young. I think loving teachings about God and Jesus gives a young child peace and comfort.)*

Soon I began my search for God in other ways.

Mom Prayed Me Here

As early as I can remember, I attended our local Methodist church regularly with Mom and Dad, Lawrence Clyde Street, and my little sister, Sandra. Every Sunday, together as a congregation, we would recite together a creed that went something like this: "God is so small he can dwell in your heart and He is so large He can fill the universe."

I wanted to stand up on the pews and shout, "That's not true. That's not who God is!" But I restrained myself. After all, I was seven years old. Who would believe me?

Almost every day I witnessed Mom pray and read her Bible, but it was several years before I learned the extent of her faith . . . and that she had dedicated me to God before I was born.

Before I came along Mom and Dad had been married seven years and were still childless. Mom yearned for a child. One day in the seventh year she reread the Old Testament account of Hannah who had also been barren for years. Finally Hannah prayed fervently to God that if He would give her a son, she would dedicate that son's life to the service of God. God honored her request and gave her a son she named Samuel:

...but Hannah had no children...And she was in bitterness of soul, and prayed unto the Lord, and wept sore.

And she vowed a vow, and said, O Lord of hosts, if thou will indeed look on the afflictions of thine handmaid, and remember me, and not forget thine handmaid, but wilt give unto thine handmaid a man child, then I will give him unto the Lord all the days of his life....

...and the Lord remembered her.

Wherefore it came to pass, when the time was come about after Hannah had conceived, that she bare a son, and called his name Samuel, saying, Because I have asked him of the Lord...

And when she had weaned him...she took him up with her...unto the house of the Lord in Shiloh: and the child was young.

For this child I prayed; and the Lord hath given me my petition which I asked of him:

Therefore also I have lent him to the Lord: as long as he liveth he shall be lent to the Lord.

(1 Samuel 1: 2, 10, 11, 19, 20, 24, 27, 28)

My mother's faith was so emboldened by this account   that she began to pray in the manner of Hannah—if Father in Heaven would remember her and grant her a child, she would raise the child in the ways of God. Not long after initiating this new level of prayer, Mom had a dream in which a heavenly being came and stood in her bedroom doorway and smiled at her. She knew that her prayers had been heard. Soon she conceived and nine months later brought me into the world.

Native American Heritage

I was born and raised in eastern Tennessee, in a town surrounded by the Great Smokey Mountains. The area around Johnson City is part of a vast area in the southeast where a portion of the Cherokee Indian Nation once resided. Legend has it that the Cherokees gave the Smokey's their name.

I remember driving to the top of the Smokey Mountains on a family picnic where we could actually look down below and see smoke-like clouds beneath us, mystically enshrouding the mountains. It was a hot summer day and I literally felt the cooling moisture on my face and arms as I ran through low-lying clouds across a meadow quilted with rhododendron bushes, wild and beautiful.

Many of my older relatives down through the years have told me that several Cherokee lines run through our family. The story goes that if a man married a Cherokee woman, she would change her name, losing her Native American heritage and identity. This was for her self-preservation.

When still a small girl, I recall watching my great grandmother Sarah Whitson Garland, after whom I was named, combing her long dark hair that flowed all the way to her feet. She had washed her tresses and was on her daughter's front porch doing a sun dry. Too young for a grasp of social graces, I said, "Grandma Garland, you are so old . . . so why is your hair so black?"

In kindness she smiled and responded, "Well, honey, that is because I have Indian blood in me."

Great Grandma Garland died at age 92 with only a few gray hairs showing around her face. In the last few years with my interest in genealogy, I have learned that Great Grandmother Sarah was a direct descendant of the great woman we call Pocahontas. That explains why as a small child, I was always drawn to the Native Americans: their music and heritage spoke deeply to my soul and sometimes, even now at times, I can perceive a Native American grandmother from ages past, calling out to me.

Great Grandma Garland was a woman who loved the Lord. Raised in the Smokey Mountains of North Carolina, she was a typical mountain woman of her day, often seen reading her Bible and chewing her snuff . . . at the same time. She led prayer meetings for those in her community and, at times, exercised healing gifts in behalf of those who were ill or "sinners." One way she displayed her love of the Lord was by spontaneously shouting praises to him with hands raised heavenward.

I remember as an eight-year-old child at our annual Decoration Day (Memorial Day) picnic watching Great Grandma praise the Lord while we decorated graves high on the windy hill of the Garland Cemetery near Baskerville, North Carolina. "What's wrong with her?" I asked my cousin Judy.

"Nothing, she's just praying," Judy replied casually as if she'd seen it many times.

And so you see I come by my spiritual gifts honestly—I inherited them through the faith of my dear mother and great grandmother.

Confusion

As I grew, I really tried to be normal. I would take part in all of the childhood games and activities and at times lose myself in friends, school activities and playing, but sooner or later I would come back to being alone with myself, thinking, searching and praying. I found confusion comparing my surroundings and experiences with what I felt in my heart. Everywhere I would find contradictions.

As an eight year-old child, I walked to and from school alone every day. One day, walking under a canopy of trees down my street, I asked God who He was. Could He really fit into my heart? Was he really larger than the universe? I didn't believe that was true. That's when a little song came into my head. I started singing aloud the words in a simple tune. *"Jesus is my Savior, God is my Father, Jesus is the Christ, but God is God of all."*

Another verse came into my mind. "*God is good, Jesus is love, God is precious, the most precious man above.*" I knew that from someplace where He lived, He looked down on me that day and gave me that little song—to teach me who He was.

In my heart, I never believed God was like a cloud or a seed. I knew he was a man with a son named Jesus. I knew he didn't live in the entire universe, but in a specific place called heaven. I knew heaven was my home and God was my Father.

When I was nine years old, I attended the funeral of my grandfather, my dad's dad. Although I had spent very little time with my grandfather, I cared for him and sensed he loved me. At his funeral I felt a great sense of peace and comfort that my grandfather was not really dead, that was just his body lying there and his spirit was with God. But all around me everywhere was confusion, people were either crying because he was dead or bitter about something that was either said or unsaid by someone in the family.

I felt very confused. Why didn't they know he was all right? God had just called him home. In my mind, I could almost see my grandfather smiling, glad to be free from the cares of this world and happy to be where he was now. As we left the funeral home, I tried to comfort my dad.

"Dad, it's all right. Grandpa Street is okay. Why are you crying so much?"

My dad turned to me and said, "I'm crying because my dad is dead and I'll never see him again. Wouldn't you cry if I died?"

In my innocent childlike way I said, "No, because I know God would take care of you."

This concerned my dad because he took this as an indication that I didn't love him, and try as I could on the way home I could not explain to him my feelings. I did love my dad, but I knew if he died he would be okay.

These kinds of experiences seemed to happen to me often. I knew and felt things inside that no one on earth had taught me, and many times as a child, it seemed that no one on earth understood me. I spent much time, even as a little child, pouring out my heart to God. At times, he seemed like my only friend.

I Felt Lonely

My teen years brought added confusion. I was beginning more and more not to fit in with the crowd. The parties and drinking I saw all around me had no appeal. I managed to grit my teeth and get through high school, but I found very little fulfillment or happiness because, well—I was just different. I had several good friends who had the same view of life, but that one part of me, the quest for answers, was my own individual cross. No one ever really understood it.

I began spending a great deal of time alone with music and found some comfort there, but the words of the songs always disappointed me in the end and left no lasting satisfaction. When I entered college, which was right across the street from my high school, I began to search for answers in books. Surely, I wasn't the only one to ever think these thoughts. With all the great philosophers down through the ages, someone must have found the answers.

I remember thinking I was getting close as I read certain poets and writers and especially pondered the poem *"Ode on Intimations of Immortality"* by William Wordsworth.

Our birth is but a sleep and a forgetting:
The Soul that rises with us, our life's Star,
Hath had elsewhere it's setting,
And cometh from afar:
Not in entire forgetfulness, And not in utter nakedness,
But trailing clouds of glory do we come From God, who is our home:
Heaven lies about us in our infancy!

After one year of college, taking many courses in many fields to find some answers, it seemed hopeless. I contemplated ending it all, either my life or my search. As I struggled within myself for answers, I decided that service to others must be the answer. A girlfriend of mine had joined VISTA, a government agency like the Peace Corps that served people in the United States. Although she served diligently, she had found very little satisfaction there. I felt my experience would be different.

My mother was beginning to feel very concerned for me. She could see that my desires were good, yet she felt my direction would only lead to heartbreak and disappointment. A prayerful woman, she spent many hours on her knees in search of answers. None came . . . except one day the Lord began to unravel a series of events which would lead me to the answers.

Peach Baskets & Laundry

At the age of 19, I was a sophomore at East Tennessee State University. I was still living at home with my parents and enjoyed the daily six-block walk to the university to attend classes and work part-time.

One morning after I had departed for the university, Mom attempted to wash some clothes when the washer broke.

As mom would tell it:

The washer just stopped...went silent. Nothing I did—checking the electrical connection, twisting the buttons, not even a good swift kick would revive it. So I filled a couple of laundry baskets, placed them in the trunk of the car, and drove a few blocks to the nearby Laundromat. It was about ten o'clock on a Monday morning, so the parking lot was almost empty, but as I pulled in I noticed a white car with Utah license plates. Visitors from Utah were pretty rare in our small town of Johnson City. I was especially intrigued because recently Sarah had been talking about majoring in social work and after graduation going to Utah to help the Indians.

As I entered the Laundromat carrying one of my baskets, there were only two other people in the room—an older couple who looked up from folding their cleaned and dried clothing with big smiles and an enthusiastic "Hello!" A warm glow radiated from their countenances.

I returned their greeting and noticed they had a very unusual laundry basket. It was a wooden peach basket painted a cheerful yellow with two wire handles. A multicolored cloth covering had been fastened around the rim of the basket and the top of the cloth was hemmed with a draw string inserted that could be pulled tight and tied in a bow to hold the clothes inside.

While making these observations, I realized I was staring. Embarrassed, I looked away, selected an empty washer and began loading my own laundry. Suddenly and without warning, a Voice spoke to my mind, "Speak to those people."

I was not surprised by the Voice...I'd heard it before. But the message was another thing. Surely the Lord knew I've always been shy around strangers. What would I say?

But the Voice persisted a second time, a bit more forcefully, "Go speak to those people." I looked their way. They had loaded their folded laundry into their peach basket and were about to leave.

I was really getting nervous when the Voice came a third time with urgency, "Go speak to those people. This is your last chance!"

I knew I had to obey. In desperation I struggled to come up with an "opener" to begin a conversation. Just as they were about to depart I walked over to the couple and said, "My, what a pretty and unusual laundry basket."

"Thank you," the lady responded. "It's from our peach orchard in Utah. We are Mormon missionaries here serving a mission for our church. I am Helen Bunnell and this is my husband, Stephen." She proceeded to describe how they had converted the peach basket into a laundry basket.

They were such friendly, nice people that I then asked, "Would you like to come to our home for dinner some evening? Our daughter, Sarah, is interested in learning more about Utah and perhaps you could help her."

"We'd be delighted to come . . . thank you."

And so began, thanks again to my mother and the Lord, another step in my spiritual journey.

I Meet the Bunnells

When I returned home from the university that evening, Mom could hardly wait to tell me of her experience at the laundry mat. She was so excited that I could learn more about Utah first hand from a couple who had lived there all their lives. I, indeed, looked forward to meeting these people who might be able to help me determine the validity of my feelings about becoming a social worker and moving to Utah to help the Indians.

The Bunnells stopped by our home that same evening and they were delightful. Stephen had a great sense of humor and Helen was truly a gracious lady. Stephen was a social worker who had worked for the state of Utah until he retired. He complimented my good intentions but kindly pointed out that there was not too much demand for social workers to help the Indians in Utah. However, he and Helen assured me if wanted to come to Utah I was welcome to stay with them in their home.

The Bunnells became good friends and visited our home often. They were happy, probably the first really happy people I had ever seen in my entire life. They seemed at peace with the world and to have a real conviction in what they were doing. We talked, or rather they asked questions and I talked.

I got the idea, very gently, that they felt the VISTA program was not for me. I agreed, and a few days later I received notice in the mail that I had not been accepted for the program. Somewhere in my heart, I was relieved, although at the same time hoping something better would come along.

They visited more and more and seemed genuinely interested in me. I remember the feeling I had as we spoke. I felt something wonderful. I felt something stirring in my soul. I had never had that particular feeling before. It was like a tide of joy and hope slowly moving over my soul, like the waves of the sea, at times strong, at times gentle, but ever present.

The Bunnells came to visit our home many times during the next six months they were in Johnson City. In fact, they lived about five blocks away in a small apartment. One cold and snowy afternoon I went for a walk, feeling very unhappy, crying and trudging off alone like someone out of "Dr. Zhivago." I picked no particular direction to walk. The snow was falling very fast as it can in the hills of Tennessee and I watched the ground as I made fresh footprints in the snow. It seemed like I walked for an hour, lost in my thoughts, searching for a better way. Why was I so different? What was I looking for? Suddenly, reality came into focus. I was standing in front of the Bunnells' apartment.

I'm not sure how I got there. Their car pulled up in front and they got out. I unloaded my heart and cried. My tears fell on the white snow. They put their arms around me and we hugged one another and talked. Soon we realized we were all cold so we went into their car and talked. I talked, they listened. They told me I was special, I was good and my desires and hopes would someday be realized. I thanked them and they took me home. In my heart, I knew that Steven and Helen Bunnell had heard me. They had heard me and understood me in a way that no one else ever had. Even though there were others in my life that cared for me, such as family, the Bunnell's seemed aware of something deep inside of me, feelings that even I did not understand about myself.

Finally, it came time for the Bunnell's to leave Johnson City, but they reiterated the invitation for me to come visit them in Utah anytime.

Launching My Spiritual Quest

Steve and Helen Bunnell were gone. Several months passed and my life was continuing to get worse. I felt as thought I could continue the quest no longer. There was nothing better out there. Everyone had to make their own way. I began to tell myself I had to get involved in life, even though it was with a group I had so resisted. If everyone smoked and drank and partied, why couldn't I? Why did I need to be so different?

I attended a few parties and tried to break the ice, but it seemed as though I was protected from some outside force to not get too involved. But it didn't help. I only felt worse. Then, I decided to give it one more try. I remembered an aunt who lived in a neighboring state. Perhaps I could go visit her, get a job and find my way there. I wrote her a letter. A few days later came the reply. She didn't feel that I should quit college at the present time. She encouraged me to stay home. It was another rejection for me and I became even more despondent.

In the meantime I had been dating a boy who was in the Marines stationed in Quantico, Virginia. He was very good to me and we had lots of fun together. When I was with him, I seemed to forget my eternal quest. Although he was not a philosopher, and we were different in many ways, I felt that I loved him. Before long he received orders to go to Vietnam. I was heartbroken. This thread of meaning I had found was taken away from me too, perhaps never to return.

When he left, it was like I hit rock bottom. I had lost my desire to search and giving up that quest made me feel and behave like a zombie. My heart was beating and my body was functioning, but the rest of me was dead. I had no desire for social contact with anyone. Going to school at the university was almost more then I could bear.

I dashed to and from my classes, never looking at anyone, never talking to anyone and with no self-esteem or self-worth. I remembered looking in my mom's vanity mirror as a little girl, how I would escape to the ceiling and almost run back to God. A feeling entered my heart that God had something special for me, if I would just hang on a little longer.

My grades in college were becoming consistently low. I would go to my room immediately after supper to study, but would usually just sit at my desk to think. One evening after sitting there for quite a while, I had a flash come out of nowhere. *Remember the Bunnells! Write them a letter and ask them if you could come to Utah and visit them.* They were now in Crossville, Tennessee, but I knew that they would soon be going back to the West. I started the letter, "You may think that I am presumptuous, but may I come to Utah to visit you?"

A few days later came a reply. As I got the letter out of the mailbox it seemed like love oozed out at the seams. As I opened it, it was in Sister Bunnell's neat and feminine handwriting, encouragingly inviting me to Utah as soon as they returned. It appeared that they actually wanted me to come and didn't feel at all that I would be a burden.

Soon I was on my way. As the plane took off and flew over the green hills of Tennessee, I hoped and prayed for a new life, a life with answers to questions I had never been able to find. On the plane ride, I sat next to a woman who asked, "Are you LDS?"

"LDS?" I asked, confused, not knowing Mormons were also called LDS (Latter-day Saints). "I'm not sure." I thought she might be asking if I had a disease similar to MS.

The Bunnell's met me at the gate with big smiles and enthusiastic hugs. They asked if before heading to their home I would like to visit one of the most famous landmarks in Utah—Temple Square. I responded, "Absolutely! I want to see it all!" My big adventure had begun.

As we drove into Salt Lake City my hosts pointed out the spires of the Salt Lake Temple with the shiny gold statue of an angel on top. We watched a beautiful film on Temple Square called *Man's Search for Happiness*. The film ends with the death of a beloved grandfather whose spirit crosses into heaven, where he is greeted by many of his deceased loved ones who are all dressed in white. That depiction of eternal life moved me to tears and was the beginning for me of a new life of spiritual experiences.

Answers

Following the Temple Square tour, we drove north to Brigham City, a peaceful little community of several thousand residents. We pulled into the driveway of a small but immaculate white, three- bedroom frame home on 300 West Street. The lush green lawn and flowers and shrubs were well-manicured, but the most striking part for me was the lot behind the house filled with an acre of peach trees loaded with little budding peaches. With frequent irrigation and tender care, by harvest time we enjoyed the largest most luscious peaches I have ever tasted. Because the supply was limited, people signed up a year in advance to reserve a bushel basket of Steve Bunnell's famous peaches.

In a back bedroom with an antique brass bed, I opened my suitcase and pulled my clothes out, carefully hanging them on the hangers in the closet. The linoleum floor was covered with a colorful handmade rug. Sister Bunnell had a petite vase she filled with fresh flowers and placed on a dresser. The white drapes hung crisp in the window as bright sunlight shone through. In this strange home, I felt like a princess in a castle. The Bunnells introduced me to their friends and family as "their Tennessee gal."

I lived in the Bunnells home only a few days when two things stood out to me. First, this couple who had been married about forty years was a model of sweet kindness to one another—they simply radiated love. Second, this couple had more clear answers to my questions about life, God and eternity than anyone I'd ever met.

The Mormon people seemed to be the happiest people I'd ever seen. They were content with their children and large families; they were always serving and reaching out to their neighbors. Mormons held weekly Sunday meetings as well as fun activities   throughout the week involving families, youth and children. Everyone thought I was special and good, therefore I wanted to be. Here the peer pressure was not to be bad, but to be good. That was the kind of peer pressure I could handle!

One night while attending an activity with the Bunnell's I was asked if I wanted to participate in a play. I accepted the offer and was assigned to play a secretary. We rehearsed for several weeks. I sang and danced on a desk on the stage, something this quiet shy girl would have never done before. After my performance, I was told I should participate in the annual Brigham City Peach Queen Contest. "It could qualify you for the Miss Utah Pageant," another member of the church told me.

I turned down the request to enter the Peach Queen Contest, but knew I loved the Mormon people. They could have more fun with Hawaiian Punch and cookies than anyone else I knew.

I always felt in my heart that God was a man, but couldn't visualize just what that meant until I started attending the Bunnells' church and learned from them that God, our Heavenly Father, is a glorified and exalted Man, who rules and governs in the heavens. His son is Jesus Christ, the same Jesus that walked the earth, now an exalted God who stands by His Father's side.

I learned we all lived with them before we were born. While there, in the Preexistence, we were trained and schooled for our earthly missions. We made friends there and some of those friends we will meet here on the earth. Those friends are called kindred spirits or eternal friends. I knew that the Bunnell's were kindred spirits to me. They had brought me something I had ached for my entire life—answers about my home in heaven before I was born. In September 1968, I was baptized a member of The Church of Jesus Christ of Latter-day Saints.

No Freeloading

My parents taught me to work hard and take care of myself. With this heritage, no way was I going to live off the Bunnells without doing my part. I first found work during the cherry harvest, something I'd never done before. I'd read *The Grapes of Wrath* and always wondered about the life of a migrant worker. I learned that it was hard and exhausting work.

In several weeks the cherries were all picked and I obtained a position on the night shift at a rest home for the elderly. It was grueling, but I needed work. My favorite "second job" that summer was out on

Highway 89 with the famous Maddox Restaurant. I worked in the drive-in division and learned to make the world's best milkshakes.

It was a great summer of new friends and new experiences, but as September rolled around my yearnings for education returned. I had promised my dad I would earn the college degree he never had the opportunity to gain. I discussed college with the Bunnell's and they encouraged me to go. Utah State University (USU) was just a half-hour drive through Sardine Canyon into Cache Valley. The problem was my minimum-wage jobs fell far short of the funds needed for tuition and books. I prayed daily for help, privately and with the Bunnells.

However, the semester soon began and I gave up hope of attending classes that fall. Then one morning I came home exhausted and ready for sleep after working a graveyard shift at the rest home. The Bunnells greeted me with their relentless enthusiasm and said, "Sarah, have some breakfast and then we're going to USU."

I knew classes had already been going for a week, but I threw on some clean clothes and away we went. I dozed in the back seat, wondering how the Bunnells imagined I could have the money for college. But they were people who had faith in God. I was about to experience another miraculous milestone in my life.

University Doors Open

Utah State University is a striking mountain campus at the mouth of majestic Logan Canyon on the east side of Cache Valley. With the autumn leaves turning, the campus and its surroundings were ablaze with color. We crossed the valley farmlands and drove up the hill to magnificent Old Main, a campus landmark with the large "A" on top symbolizing the university's beginnings as an "agricultural" college. To this day they are called the "Aggies."

At the Bunnells' invitation I climbed out of the car, hiding my fatigue behind a big smile of anticipation. As we walked up the steps and through the doors, I admired the pristine preservation of that grand old building. Soon we were in the financial aid office and the Bunnells were pleading my cause to the secretary. A kind- faced, white-haired man stepped forward from a back office and introduced himself as the director. He invited us to join him in his office where he listened intently to my story.

My sincere desires to continue my education must have come across because he finally said, "Earlier this morning a student who had been awarded a grant and loan to attend USU this year notified me she could not come. Since school has already started, I was pondering what to do with the money. I feel impressed to give it to you."

I was stunned. I smiled so big it hurt. Our prayers were answered. Before we left campus that day I was fully enrolled for fall semester at USU. Furthermore, a couple of professors who commuted daily from Brigham City to the university offered to let me ride with them. I was no longer tired and almost too excited to sleep that night.

More Miracles

It seemed that ever since I met the Bunnells, miracles and spiritual experiences increased in my life. First came the miraculous way my mother was guided to speak to them and invite them to our home. Then there were the impressions that I should accept the Bunnells' invitation and go to Utah, which I temporarily ignored and paid the price. Next was the profound experience in the *Man's Search for Happiness* film where I received a powerful personal witness that we truly are eternal beings. And then the Bunnells' faith added to my prayers that led to my miraculous enrollment at USU. I soon learned this was only the beginning.

That first semester at USU I made many new friends. A group of five girls invited me to move in with them in the apartment they were renting just a couple blocks off campus. During Spring Break two of these girls took me to meet their families and see the farmlands of southern Utah. On the drive back, as we emerged from the canyon and the university came into sight across the valley, a distinct message came into my mind. *"Soon you will meet the man you are going to marry."* My ability to recognize the voice of the Spirit of God was growing, and I marveled that it would be so.

A month or so later I was going down the steps leaving the education building. Dozens of students were coming and going in close quarters during the ten-minute break between classes, but when I brushed the arm of a certain young man I suddenly felt something unique as the Spirit whispered to my mind, *"There goes the man you will someday marry."*

I whirled around for a look, but he was already disappearing into the crowd. All I could tell from the back was he was about my height and had gorgeous dark wavy hair. I also brushed that thought off as indigestion. I mean really, what a strange thought!

Brent Finds Me

During my second semester I was enjoying school, happily living with girlfriends near campus, and working part-time in the Foreign Students Office. Then one Sunday in April I was asked to give a short talk in church. I did not know him yet, but Brent attended. He was intrigued and cleverly learned my name from the program.

The next afternoon I was walking toward home from my last class when someone called my name. "Sarah . . ."

I looked to the source and saw a guy across the street in a white car. "Sarah, would you like a ride home?" he asked.

I promptly looked straight ahead and continued walking. I was well-trained—no good Southern girl was going to talk to strangers, let alone accept a ride from one.

"Sarah . . . may I give you a ride?" he persisted.

I couldn't believe it. Who was this guy? Couldn't he take a hint? I looked straight ahead and doubled my speed. By this time several students were watching the scene with some amusement.

Suddenly I was startled by a white blur at my side. The stranger had actually made a U-turn and was creeping along next to me. What was I going to do? A third time I heard that obnoxious voice even louder. "Sarah, may I give you a ride home?"

The curious crowd of students was growing. This was getting embarrassing. I whirled around toward the car with my most potent "Back off, Turkey!" look . . . and realized I'd seen this guy at church. He had caught my eye on more than one occasion because he was older—maybe around 26—and I'd heard he was a graduate student.

With the obnoxious persistence he'd already manifested, I figured the only way to shut him up was to cooperate. So I swallowed my Southern pride and climbed into the front seat with the cute stranger. With embarrassment, I noticed that some of the students high-fived each other—and I realized the cute stranger had gorgeous dark wavy hair.

"Hi. My name is Brent," he said as he extended his hand. I shook his hand and he continued, "I know your name is Sarah from the church program. I enjoyed your talk in Sunday School." "Thanks," I mumbled, withdrawing my hand and still not sure what I'd gotten myself into.

"Which way home?" asked Mr. Persistent.

I gave directions to my nearby apartment and within about two minutes we pulled into my parking lot overlooking Cache Valley.

An Unexpected Conversation

We sat in the front seat of his white Mercury Meteor, and I was still apprehensive about what I was doing there. As a child, because of my mother's overprotective nature, I was told to sit on the porch while the neighborhood kids played ball in the street. I was never allowed to join them, and I had accepted this view of life—to play it safe and follow all the rules. Yet here I was, sitting with a man in a car in broad daylight, a man that I hadn't been properly introduced to—in the Southern way.

But I was 20 years old now, over 2,000 miles away from my parents' home and I was willing to try this, although I did keep my hand on the door handle of his car, knowing a single twist of the handle would propel me out the door to run if necessary.

"Where are you from?" Brent asked. "Tennessee," I replied.

"Well, I guessed you were somewhere from the South because of your accent."

"I've been trying to tone that down so people can understand me, but it's not easy," I said, a bit embarrassed.

My Southern accent had been somewhat of a plague for me since arriving in Utah. In Tennessee I spoke like everyone else and dressed like everyone else. In Utah, I stood out simply by the way I said "Hello."

A few cruel people had asked, "You're from Tennessee? Do people wear shoes there? Does your dad make moonshine?" I needed to drop my Tennessee image and I needed to drop it fast.

"I'm a junior studying elementary education. What about you?" I asked, enunciating my words with the effort of a spinster English teacher.

Brent replied, "I'm a graduate student working on my Ph.D. as a psychologist."

"That's interesting," I said while making a mental note to look up the word psychologist in the dictionary when I was safely inside my apartment.

"I enjoyed your talk in church," he said. "Something happened while you were speaking. I saw a light, a very bright golden light around your head and shoulders. I have never seen anything like that before in my life."

"Really?" I asked in surprise. Either this was the best pick-up line I'd ever heard or Brent was telling the truth. He continued to speak about the experience with much sincerity. I understood that God could manifest things in many different ways, and if Brent had seen my spiritual aura, then he must understand spiritual things like me.

What started out as a conversation about school and weather turned into something more. He told me he'd recently returned from spending two-and-a-half years serving as a missionary in Mexico. He loved the people, serving the poorest of the poor. He said adjusting to life back in the United States had been difficult because he'd wanted to stay longer in Mexico.

I told him how I felt God had a plan for me, how my mother had heard a voice when she met the Bunnells in the laundry mat, and how I ended up in Utah. I also told Brent about the miracles in my life, how I'd had no money or job, but now I was a full-time student and employed on the student faculty.

Brent then shared with me that while on his mission he had prayed with a poor widow who later shared with him that during the prayer she'd opened her eyes and saw an angel standing between him and his companion. This fascinated me. I wholeheartedly believed it. Before I knew it, we were talking about the unseen world, heaven and angels. Time stood still. Instantly I had a spiritual bond with this man. I looked out the car window and my heart soared as I marveled at the personal experiences we'd just shared.

As a Southern girl, I knew to never overextend my time with anyone. I was very aware that our time together should come to a close and I understood a gracious exit was in order, so I finally turned the handle of the car door, quickly thinking of an excuse as to why I needed to leave so fast. I decided to impress him with my culinary skills. I said, "I'm making dinner for my roommates (which was actually Kraft macaroni and cheese) and need to get inside to *bowl* water."

"*Bowl* water?" Brent asked with a twinkle in his eye. "What's that?"

"Well, I'm making dinner and need to start with *bowled* water." I was trapped again in my world of thick Southern drawl. Looking into his dark brown eyes, I couldn't stay focused on my determination to sound like I'd lived in Utah my entire life.

"Do you mean boil?" Brent asked, and I knew he was teasing me. My Southern grace was quickly dissolving like sugar in bowled, I mean boiled water.

As I shut the car door and started walking up the stairs to my apartment, I suddenly sensed why Brent had taken an interest in me. I supposed I was his new case study and he would probably write his dissertation about the strange girl from the hills of Tennessee, her unusual language and her quirky mannerisms.

Tennis

A week later, the phone rang and my roommate answered. She started laughing and giggling and I knew she was talking with a guy. About ten minutes later, she hollered down the hall, "Sarah, the phone's for you. It's Brent." It appeared I wasn't the only girl interested in Brent Hinze

Brent asked if I'd like to play tennis the next afternoon after class. I thought it would be nice to have a friend like him, so I agreed, ignoring the little voice in my head reminding me that he probably needed more documentation for his research on the inner workings of my mind.

The next day, I saw him pull up and park outside my apartment window. I was ready to go, wearing yellow shorts and a striped yellow-turquoise shirt. Without hesitation, I ran out the front door, eager to see him. I found it ironic; the last time I saw him I was trying to figure out how to run away from him, and now I was excited to run into another encounter with him.

We arrived at the tennis court and he handed me an extra racquet he'd brought. I was geared up, ready to go as I laced up my white tennis shoes. Really, how hard could tennis be? He would go easy on me.

We took our places at opposite ends of the court when I heard a *ping* as Brent's ball hit the strings of the racket.

When I tried to hit the ball back, I heard a *thud*, as my ball hit the wood frame of my racket. Back and forth we went, but rarely did the ball I hit land back on Brent's side of the court. Always the gentleman, Brent agreed to collect the balls that were quickly gathering in the far left field. About 15 minutes into our rally, his friend Lane arrived at the courts and stopped for a brief conversation.

"Hey, Brent, we should get together and play in the next few days," Lane said.

"Why don't you two play now and I'll watch," I mercifully suggested, knowing these two competitive males would most likely take the bait.

I sat on the bleachers and watched. It was fun for a while to watch them slug it out, but after a while I decided I'd seen enough and walked back to my apartment. About an hour later, there was a knock on my door. It was Brent.

"Would you like to go with me to the movies tomorrow night?" he asked.

"Sure," I said, happy to have a nice new friend in this strange new land of Utah.

The following night, I saw him pull up again in front of my apartment. I was wearing a red skirt and a beautiful white blouse with rows of ruffles. I had purchased it as a Valentines gift to myself, because I hadn't had a Valentine that year. I took one last look in the mirror and adjusted the belt around my waist.

I opened the door and was taken aback by the man standing in front of me. Where before I had seen friendship—I now saw shoulders.

Brent's body language oozed strength through strong muscular shoulders and a confident stature.

I had wondered whether courtesy was his thing, based on his obnoxious perseverance the day we first met. He later told me he didn't know what had come over him that day. He had never been so bold before or since.

We descended the steps to his car and Brent opened the door for me. Then something happened I'd never experienced or even expected. Before starting the car, he asked if we could pray together. Of course I agreed, and then I marveled as he thanked God for the opportunity to enjoy this time together. He prayed we would get to know one another better, travel and return from our date in safety. I was touched. As we drove to the movie I thought, "Who is this guy? Is he for real?" I had prayed for a spiritual guy to come into my life. Was this him?

The movie was fine, but my focus was on this guy next to me. I kept hoping he would hold my hand, and finally he did. What a feeling as his fingers laced into mine!

On the way home we stopped at the Arctic Circle restaurant for the world's second-best milkshakes. We returned to my apartment and Brent turned off the engine. The view of the valley below with lights sparkling in the night was a definite assist to a budding romance.

We soon entered my apartment and my roommates were conveniently absent. Brent noticed my guitar sitting in the corner.

"Can you play me something?" he asked.

I had started to wonder if there was anything I could do better than this guy. Maybe it was the guitar.

I sat on the couch and started strumming the song of my mountain people, "Little Brown Jug." I hit a crescendo at the climax of the song, "She loved gin and he loved rum, and ho ho ho they had lots of fun," while Brent graciously listened with his head turned to the side.

When I finished, he held his arms out, implying he would like a turn plucking around on the old guitar. He spent a moment tuning the strings. How had I not noticed how out of tune it was?

Wouldn't you know it, he played a rendition of the classical score *Malaguena*.

"Wow, that's pretty good," I said, a little dumbfounded. Brent seemed to do everything grandiose.

I took the guitar out of his hands and slid it behind the door before he could do any more damage, then I pulled one of my favorite books off my bookshelf, *The Prophet* by Kahlil Gibran. Brent took the book out of my hand.

"This is one of my favorite books," he said and haphazardly opened it to a page with a poem on marriage. He read the entire passage, during which a beautiful feeling came into the room. Once again, we were discussing things of heaven, feeling close to God as we continued learning more about each other.

Brent looked at the clock. "It's midnight," he said, and I stood up to walk him to the door. He walked over to me and unexpectedly, gave me a gentle kiss. The kiss, tender and sweet, set the stage for a whole new relationship with Brent, and I marveled at this new man in my life.

Memories Rekindled

The next day of our magical first week was Saturday. That afternoon Brent invited me on a drive up Logan Canyon, which manifests some of the most majestic views imaginable. We turned our heads this way and that to peer up at castle-like rock walls and nearly perpendicular hillsides punctuated with stands of pine.

After about half an hour we had "oooed and aahed" our way up the narrow twisting road until we reached a mountain pass with a straight stretch of highway across the summit.

We parked the car near a shady meadow alive with wildflowers, surrounded by groves of white birch. Brent took my hand as we walked. An impression softly settled upon me: *I had known this man before. I had walked with him in heaven.*

A remembrance of this came from deep in my soul and began to fill my heart. It reminded me of an experience I'd had within days of arriving in Utah when I was sitting on the front lawn with my new girlfriend, Mavis. As we looked into the darkness of the evening sky watching for shooting stars, she turned to me and said, "You know we lived in heaven with God before we were born."

I'd sat in silence, amazed at how easily she said something I had only believed in the deepest most sacred place of my heart. This was the first time I'd heard another person say that we lived with God before we were born. All my life I had known it was true, but here with this new Mormon friend, she shared it like it was common knowledge. This impacted me greatly. I had found people that believed as I did, that life has no beginning and no end.

So, here I was walking with Brent thinking about my heavenly home. The scenery, the sounds, the smells—it all seemed so familiar. The feeling became sacred then, and we were quiet, almost reverent, and we didn't speak for a time. Finally I broke the silence. In an unusual display of boldness I said, "I think I have walked with you before in heaven before we were born."

"I feel it too," Brent whispered, drawing me close in his strong arms. From that moment, we sensed one another as we had in the world before we were born and our spirits renewed a relationship from long ago. We could feel there had been love between us before and a divine spark now mysteriously rekindled that love and those memories as we strolled hand in hand on a picturesque mountaintop that reached toward heaven.

Eventually it was time to drive back down the canyon and return to the real world. As we drove across campus as evening descended, our magical first week was coming to a close. Our surroundings looked the same, but we were not.

We saw each other every day for the next two weeks.

Horse Rider or Not

One day Brent invited me to his parent's ranch in North Logan. His family had horses and he wanted us to go on a ride out in the pasture land surrounding the ranch. I had romanticized about horses all of my life, how beautiful and strong they were, but I had never ridden one except a few times when I was a child. On one occasion my parents had placed me on a pony that was strapped to a small turn wheel, and I went around and around in the same place with a handler actually holding the bridle for me.

Brent was athletic and fearless in his zest for life, but my Southern upbringing and my mother's fears and insistence that I never be involved in athletics had left me afraid of anything that involved risk. However, despite my restricted past, I wanted to impress Brent and show him I could play in his world.

He finished saddling the horses and motioned me over to hop on. I stood next to the saddled-up horse as he showed me which foot to put in the stirrup. I looked at his rugged cowboy boots next to my bobby socks and white sneakers and knew I had a ways to go to fit in.

"I didn't realize horses were so big," I said, as I stood next to this gigantic horse.

"Just don't stand too close to his mouth," Brent said, pointing to the head of the horse. "My dad once saw a woman get her nose bit off by a horse at a county fair."

"Good to know," I thought as I mounted the horse. I barely had time to grab the reins before Brent patted the rear of the horse and away I went! The horse took off to a small creek when I noticed how low the tree branches were. I ducked my head as twigs and leaves pulled at my hair. My feet were stuck in the stirrups and I had no way of dismounting—not that I'd want to jump off a speeding horse anyway—but if it meant living instead of dying, I would do it.

Closer to the creek, the branches grew thicker and lower. I probably would have been decapitated at any moment, but like a Western movie hero, Brent appeared at my side and took my horse's reins in his hands.

"Whoa," he said to the horse and it instantly obeyed his command. Brent jumped off his horse and took my shaking hand. With his help, I managed to get off my horse and took comfort in his arms.

"Are you all right?" he asked, pulling a tangled twig out of my hair.

What could I say to him? I hate your horse? I hate this creek with all of its enormous trees? I would say nothing, but bask in the strength of his comforting embrace. I couldn't pretend I fit into his world at all, but I couldn't deny I was falling in love with this man.

A Choir of Angels

I had known Brent for only ten days, yet I was falling in love. After another date, we parked at my apartment and gazed out again at the beautiful evening vision of Logan, Utah. Our feelings were growing as we talked about things of the heart.

"Last night when I left you," Brent said, "I went home and walked back to the pasture and just looked up to the heavens and thanked God for you. You have brought something special to me, something that I have needed for a long time."

"What have I given you?" I asked, not so much fishing for a compliment, but trying myself to understand this magic that was happening between us.

"Being with you makes me feel closer to God," he said. "All of my life I have studied His word and I have tried to serve Him, but part of me has always felt alone and isolated, until now. I don't feel alone anymore."

I knew what he meant. My heart was also filling up with a peace I had never known. It was as if I had found the other half of my soul, a part of me that had been lost since I had come to earth.

"Let's have prayer," Brent said, "to thank God for bringing us together."

Brent took my hand and began to pray. "Our dear Heavenly Father, we thank you for this beautiful spring night and we thank you for each other."

He continued to pray. I listened to the strength of his deep voice and his articulate choice of words. After all, this was a Ph.D. praying. I marveled that I was here with him, and with a faith that brought me closer to the God I loved.

The sound of singing caught my ear, very faint at first but gradually growing stronger. It sounded like a church choir, because the tone of the music was like a heavenly hymn.

As Brent continued to pray, I wondered why my roommates were playing church music so late at night. They had never played records of the Mormon Tabernacle Choir, or any other choir, and unless the windows were open, we couldn't have heard it outside anyway.

The music became clearer and I no longer strained to hear it. A large choir of voices sang glory to God. I was given an understanding in my heart and mind that caused me to burst into tears. Language failed me as I tried to understand what I was experiencing.

Brent quickly finished the prayer and asked, "What's wrong?"

"Do you hear it?" I asked.

"Hear what?" Brent whispered.

I struggled to get any words out of my mouth. For this experience, there were no words. Finally, I gathered my thoughts.

"It's a choir of angels. They are singing praises to God. I think they are singing because we are together."

He held me as I cried and a moment later I could no longer hear them singing. I needed to wait a few more years before I would more fully understand the meaning of this heavenly choir.

Butterscotch Pie

My mother had schooled me in the arts of a Southern woman.

She taught me such important rules as:

You never speak to a man unless you are formally introduced.

You never call a man unless you are engaged or married.

The way to a man's heart is through his stomach.

While my mom and dad were dating, my mother invented her trademark accessory—butterscotch pie. She created her own recipe. The butterscotch pudding always stood so proud in the pie crust with little droplets of brown sugar rising to the top of the creamy confection. She served it to Dad throughout their courtship, but after they were married, apparently, the pies started to slow down a bit.

My dad—seeing the crisis at hand—conjured up a grand story about his health. He said, "The doctors are concerned that I have a tendency to lose weight. If you, Edna, my sweet wife, would continue with the butterscotch pies often, I would be spared the lingering illness."

Being a sweet Southern woman, with a large dose of naïveté, my mother bought the story—hook, line, and sinker.

Therefore, I grew up with Mom, a devoted homemaker, grinding out the pies regularly until somewhere along the line Dad finally confessed he'd been teasing her about the whole weight loss and lingering illness thing. The idea that he could tease her for so many years caused Dad to just love

Mom even more. I grew up with this love story between my parents, and it allowed me to acquire some helpful hints of my own in the dating department.

The day came when I baked Brent his first butterscotch pie. It wasn't easy making a pie in a student apartment, but I managed. He liked it and commented that it was tasty.

I teasingly replied, "Sand can be tasty!" We ended up having a flour-throwing party in the kitchen and chased each other around the table before hurriedly cleaning up our mess before my roommates came home.

A Haunting Melody

A few years earlier, while still in Tennessee as a sophomore in college, I was exposed to classical music through a course in music appreciation. My parents were not musically inclined, so the course opened my eyes to a world of music I had never known.

One day the professor played for us Tchaikovsky's *Piano Concerto #1*. It stirred within me an indescribable feeling. I cried, experiencing loneliness—almost abandonment. The dramatic music was racing and seemed to explode at every turn.

Just when I thought I could contain how I felt, another stanza seemed to force more emotion from my heart. It was the music of love and war, birth and death. I was stretched. Although raw, the music was full with grandeur and a hope that was impossible to contain.

Later that day while riding the city bus toward home, I intentionally passed my usual stop and went to a record store where I purchased a record of *Piano Concerto #1*. Much to the frustration of my mother, I played that piece over and over again, seeking to discover why I was so drawn to this haunting melody.

I left Tennessee and moved to Utah the following summer, and still had no clue as to why *Piano Concerto #1* touched me so. Then during the second week after I met Brent, we were meandering around campus one evening when he suggested we go to the music building. Upon entering the building we were met by a disharmony of sounds coming from a corridor of small rooms in which students were practicing a variety of musical instruments. We searched and found an empty practice room with a piano. We entered, closed the door and Brent sat down at the piano. Not only was I surprised to discover he played, I was stunned when he began passionately playing his favorite piece, Tchaikovsky's *Piano Concerto #1*.

That beautiful melody once again stirred something within me, only this time there was something more. As Brent played, I was enveloped in déjà vu. I recalled hearing and loving that music in heaven before I was born. But now, with Brent playing it, the melody no longer evoked loneliness, but a sense of eternal truth.

Years later, I found a quote that almost perfectly expressed my feelings that day:

Sometimes during solitude, I hear truth
Spoken with clarity and freshness:
Uncolored and untranslated, it speaks
from within myself in a language
Original but inarticulate,
Heard only with the soul,
And I realized I brought it with me,
Was never taught it,
Nor can I effectively teach it to another.
— Hugh B. Brown

The Proposal

Despite our immediate attraction to each other, Brent and I dated for almost a year before he finally popped the question. He wanted to do something spectacular and propose when we sang in a student choir on Salt Lake City Temple Square, but he lost his nerve.

After all, he was a confirmed bachelor and seven years my senior—I was 21 and he was 28. So it took real guts for him to propose to me, even after all the witnesses we'd had that God wanted us together.

Earlier in the relationship Brent had said, "I can't . . . I won't tell you that I love you, even though I do, until saying it will never hurt you."

I thought this must be a psychologist thing. I, on the other hand, wanted to tell him I loved him, but I held back for fear that it would be too bold. After all, I couldn't make the first move—it wouldn't be right. So we dated and dated, month after month, while I prayed to endure the process, and yes, the game of it all.

Finally, one afternoon I made a picnic lunch for us to possibly take up to the canyon again. At this time, I was in my final semester of college and the president of my women's study group in my singles ward at church. So I was very busy in addition to seeking a happy solution to the dating game.

I packed the homemade sandwiches and treats into an old-fashioned picnic basket, red-checkered cloth and all. I was wearing a cute dress with a floral scarf around my neck when Brent arrived for lunch. His time was short that day, so we decided to spread a blanket on the back lawn and enjoy our picnic there.

Over the past few months I'd been reading a book given to me on my 20th birthday by Sister Bunnell. The book, *Fascinating Womanhood,* was written decades earlier. Some might claim it to be outdated and old-fashioned, but I read it with great intrigue. The author illustrated how feminine qualities in a woman's clothing, her voice, and her mannerisms encourage a man to be more masculine.

I spread the homemade quilt and took the lunch out of the picnic basket. I adjusted my lace apron around my waist and waited for Brent to speak.

"Look at you," he said. "You're beautiful, and who cares about lunch. I just want to take you in my arms."

I smiled and reflected on my interview the day before with a school official from Pocatello, Idaho. I had signed up to take part in job interviews for their school district. Before I left for the interview, I made sure to leave Brent a note on his apartment door, telling him the time, the building, as well as the room number. His roommate Paul had found it first and called the psychology building to give Brent the message. I was hoping this would wake him up to the fact that I was moving on with my life if he didn't get his act together and propose to me.

I arrived at the designated location, and the district official soon called my name. I joined him in a room and the interview went well. He seemed impressed with my grades and my responses. I had just read a book about a Teacher of the Year that ran a very innovative classroom, and I shared these ideas with him. I fully expected the man to offer me a contract on the spot.

Suddenly when there was a loud firm knock on the door. The interviewer paused, got up, opened the door and went outside. He soon returned with a look of disappointment on his face and said, "It's your boyfriend, Brent. He wants to talk to you."

I nodded, then went out the door with a serious professional demeanor and met Brent's eyes.

"What's going on?" I asked with polite smile.

"What are you doing?" Brent asked. "Don't . . . don't even think about signing a contract."

"Why not?" I asked, as strong as a lion, yet as meek as a kitten. "I have to figure out how to take care of myself when I graduate."

Brent looked at me and sighed. "Well, I have some other ideas of how to take care of you."

"What ideas?" I continued, keeping my smile subdued.

"Let's have lunch tomorrow and we'll talk," he said anxiously.

"I have to catch up on some data with my dissertation today. I just ran over here in a gallop from the psychology lab."

I watched as the perspiration dripped down his forehead. By now I had let go of the thought that he was just studying me as part of a project. I knew he was in love, but pretty soon he was going to have to fess up.

Now on the picnic blanket, he looked so innocent. His defenses were finally collapsing.

"What are we going to do?" he asked. "You have already had an interview for teaching school next year in Idaho and I convinced you to not sign any contracts. More schools are going to want you. Tell me what you want me to do. I love you."

I held those words in my heart and let them glisten and sparkle, like a beautiful diamond in the sunlight.

"I love you too and I want to marry you," I said with a boldness I would never apologize for. We'd been dating for 51 weeks. I knew it was now or never.

"If we get engaged now, we could have a short engagement and get married in June," Brent suggested. "Do you think we could get a wedding planned and ready by June?"

I closed my eyes for a second and felt a gentle sigh of relief wash over me.

"Do you think you're ready to marry?" he asked. I opened my eyes and answered with a smile.

Brent had to get back to campus, so we were still not engaged, but we were one step closer to getting there.

That evening, before darkness set in, Brent called and asked if I wanted to go into town with him. I was literally holding a toilet scrubber when he called and had the attire on to match. I was willing to go into town with him, but I didn't have time to clean up and change clothes (although I did take out my curlers and brush out my hair). This was how I dressed when I cleaned house. Take it or leave it.

At this time, I was living in a beautiful home with a roommate whose parents were in Bolivia serving an LDS mission. Brent knocked on the front door and when he saw me, looked cautiously at my casual attire. "Are you ready to go?" he asked, not certain if I really wanted to be seen like that in public or not.

"You bet," I said and took off my yellow rubber gloves.

We walked to his car in the driveway. He slowed down and turned to me with a cautious look on his face. I wasn't sure what he was thinking.

"I'm ready when you are," he said with a subdued look like a wild animal who was in the process of being tamed. Was he talking about going into town or getting married? I turned, put my hand on my hip and said, "If that's a proposal, you better get down on your knees and do it right."

He took my hand and walked me around to the driver's side of the car. He opened the car door and I slid inside, placing my hands on the steering wheel. He took my hand off the wheel and knelt down in the road.

"I love you, Sarah," he said. "I'm ready. Will you marry me? I want to make our relationship eternal."

Finally, after one year of being a case study, a friend, a failure at tennis and horseback riding, he had proposed! I had a fiancé I loved and wanted to be with, just as much as he loved and wanted to be with me.

"Of course, of course," I said as his lips pressed down on mine. He slid in the car and I scooted over to the passenger seat. Now his hands were on the steering wheel.

I.Q. and Endurance Test

Sometimes Brent was Brent, but other times he was Dr. Hinze, psychologist. He was in one of his moods, fresh off his latest research bandwagon and ready to hook me up to his brain reader. The only thing missing was the metal cap dome and the wires. Okay, what really happened was Brent took me across campus to the psychology building. "Let's go into my office today and do a little test," he suggested.

"All right," I said, ever trusting of my new fiancé.

"I'm learning to conduct I.Q. tests and need some more practice," he said.

I knew it. I had sensed that eventually the day would come when I would be his patient, but I knew he loved me, so I was game. Like riding a horse, I had another hurdle to cross.

Ever the professional, Dr. Hinze sat at his desk, giving instructions while I sat in a student's chair sharpening my #2 pencil. I was a little nervous.

It was the longest fill-in-the-blank test I'd ever taken. What felt like most of the day was only two hours, but I was with my sweetheart, I didn't care.

At some points, Brent concentration to not get lost in his deep dreamy voice, but with a little effort I stayed focused. He showed my different puzzle arrangements I had to fit together. He timed me as I discerned different pattern designs.

Just when I thought I was done, I had a page of vocabulary words to define. Finally, I finished and it took Brent 20 minutes to score the results. I sat and sweat. What would he do if I scored low? Would it matter if I brought a low I.Q. into his gene pool? I waited for a hint of a smile, but Dr. Hinze was so serious.

Finally, he turned and I recognized Brent again. "Geez, you scored a 142!" he said.

Later in the week, Brent had another idea. I had passed his mental test and now he wanted to understand my physical endurance. I felt like an astronaut being qualified to go to the moon.

Maybe Brent just wanted to have some fun with me, but I still felt a little insecure about the whole doctor thing. We meet up with Brent's friend Larry and his fiancé in Provo and parked near "Y" mountain, a steep mountain east of Provo. I had never owned a pair of athletic shoes, let alone hiking boots, so again I wore my little white sneakers and bobby socks. We didn't bring water and I was wearing long pants. I had no idea what I was in for.

The day was hot. We started the hike, moving through the brush on a well-worn dirt path. Parts were so steep that I was a little scared. I'd never done anything like this before. Hiking through Logan Canyon had been like heaven, but "Y" Mountain made me want to run home and hide underneath my blankie.

As we neared the top, I noticed how dry my mouth was. Brent, Larry and his fiancé started to cheer. I, on the other hand, was saving my energy for the hike back down, dreaming of root beer, a favorite Mormon beverage. Half way back down, my legs felt like wet noodles. Every step I took, my legs grew weaker and weaker.

About 100 feet from the bottom, Brent noticed my condition and told me to jump on his back. With my arms wrapped around his neck I rested my head on top of his black wavy hair while he took the final steps to the car.

"How about a root beer float?" he said, as he helped me into the passenger seat.

I smiled. Brent knew hiking the mountain had been hard for me, but I was proud I could do it. This man was going to encourage me to step out of my bubble and do things I had never imagined. I felt exhilarated!

We drove through town and I let the wind cool me off. Mormons like root beer and in Provo, every road corner had a gas station and a root beer stand. We stopped at the first one we saw. After I finished my root beer float, I went to the soda counter and asked for a refill. I was still thirsty.

I Wanted Children

One evening, Brent and I were sitting in his apartment discussing the last plans for the wedding. The invitations had been sent, flowers and cake were ordered and we could hardly believe how fast our wedding day was approaching. Very soon, we would start our lives together.

While standing in the kitchen making last-minute wedding arrangements, I felt I needed to discuss something—birth control, or the lack of it.

"Brent, I want you to know my doctor is not sure if I can ever have children, but I feel in my heart that everything will be all right. I want to have a child right away. I want God to plan when our children come."

He looked at me and said with a twinkle in his eyes, "Whatever you want."

Our Wedding Day

I soon called my parents and told them the good news. They were happy for me, and we began to make arrangements. Our marriage would take place on June 3, which would work out well, since my parents were already coming out for my graduation on June 6. The week before the wedding, Brent and I spent time with my parents, showing them the sights of Logan, taking them to USU, and having a barbecue at the Bunnells. Everyone seemed to really like each other.

My parents, my sister and I were all staying at the Bunnells. The morning of June 3, I was up at 4 a.m., which wasn't a problem because I'd been too excited to sleep anyway. A few days earlier, my mom and I had gone dress shopping, looking for the perfect dress to wear to the temple. We had found a garden green dress covered with pink, orange and yellow flowers. My wedding dress that I would put on later, was tucked inside a gray plastic garment bag hanging in my closet. I had bought it at a little dress shop in Logan before my parent's had arrived. It was the second dress I tried on and had a price tag of $59. My parents had given me a budget of $500 for the wedding.

I so respected their generosity, knowing how hard my dad worked and how careful my mom was with money. I knew this $59 dress would be perfect. At 4:30 a.m., I applied my make-up and gently combed the curls of my long blonde hair. I would wear my hair down knowing that's how Brent liked it best too. I tiptoed into the kitchen for some water. I was too nervous to eat.

Brent's parents had sold the ranch months earlier and had moved to Layton in a beautiful home. At 5:30 a.m., my parents and I packed into the Bunnell's car and started the drive down to Layton to meet up with Brent and his parents. At 6:30 a.m., we arrived in Layton. Brent was in the driveway, dressed in a dark suit. He picked up his luggage and was putting it in the trunk of *The White Charger*. That man would be my husband!

"Oh, look at him," I said. "He's so handsome."

Sister Bunnell turned to me and said, "Sarah, always look at him that way and you will have a wonderful marriage."

We started the caravan to the Salt Lake City Temple. When we arrived, my parents and Brent's sisters waited outside the temple while Brent and I went inside. Along with his parents and a small group of family and friends, we gathered in the sealing room. An apostle of the church, N. Eldon Tanner, was scheduled to seal us. Upon his arrival, he invited Brent and me to kneel at the altar. Dressed in white, in a beautiful room glowing with chandelier light, and with God and angels as our witnesses, it was pronounced that we were man and wife.

After the sealing, a temple matron directed me down a long hallway, pointing the way back to the bridal dressing room. Always a bit directionally impaired, I unknowingly took a wrong turn. At the end of the hallway, I stood in front of a large ornate door, beautiful enough to be on the front of a castle. Could this be the entrance into the bridal dressing room?

I opened the door and found myself standing outside on an upper porch of the temple, looking over the beautiful grounds. Clearly, I had taken a wrong turn, but I took a moment alone, holding dear to the fact that I was now Mrs. Sarah Hinze, married to the most wonderful man in the world.

Later, I was told my dad had been on the temple grounds waiting for Brent and me to exit, when he started crying.

"Look there," he said to my mom and Brent's sisters. "There's an angel standing outside, near the top of that temple."

"That's not an angel," Brent's sister replied. "That's Sarah."

My parents had perfect trust in my decision to move to Utah, to become Mormon, and to marry Brent in a sacred ceremony in the LDS temple. My dad thought I was an angel——my joy was full.

The Honeymoon

We honeymooned at Bear Lake, a small lakeside town an hour's drive from Logan. My parents had flown out from Tennessee and were staying with the Bunnells in Brigham City. Although it was our honeymoon, we felt an obligation to hurry back to be good hosts to my parents. So we packed our bags and drove back through scenic Logan Canyon, stopping briefly for another memorable walk through the meadow where we had our déjà vu experience—where we had walked and talked and felt love like this before…long ago in a heavenly meadow.

Arriving in Brigham City, we were greeted by my parents, the Bunnells, and Jim and Marilyn Madsen, next door neighbors who had also become good friends. My dad had a delightful sense of humor and we enjoyed a good laugh over his reaction when I called home to announce my engagement. "Mom, Dad, guess what? I'm engaged to be married to that guy I told you about, Brent Hinze."

Dad had responded, "Hinze? With a name like that, what is he, a German cowboy?"

I chuckled and explained, "He does come from a western family with a veterinarian father, has spent time on his grandparents' ranch and is a good horseman, but now he is working on a Ph.D. in psychology."

That last statement made my parents nervous. Dad was an intelligent man, but he always felt a little uncomfortable around people with degrees. Because of circumstances beyond his control, dad never received the college education he wanted. So when they flew to Utah, Dad was a little anxious to meet Brent, who was about to become a doctor, and Brent's father was also a doctor. But Brent's family was as gracious and "down home" as could be. I was grateful when my parents whispered to me how comfortable and welcome they were made to feel.

However, the biggest compliment was yet to come. For our honeymoon Brent and I took my parents around to Utah historical sites. Brent and my parents hit it off beautifully. Brent quickly picked up on Dad's humor, and Mom and I laughed constantly as they joked in friendly banter. When it was time for my parents to fly back to Tennessee, Dad whispered in my ear, "You know I was nervous about meeting Brent who is about to earn his Ph.D., but he's great . . . he's just like talking to a high school drop-out."

To this day Brent insists, "That's one of the highest compliments I ever received."

My parents wanted to hold an open house in their Tennessee home to honor the newlyweds. We weren't sure if *The White Charger* would make the nearly five thousand mile round trip. And besides, my parents advised that with the many relatives and friends they expected to celebrate our marriage, we would need a bigger car to hold all the loot we would receive. Fortunately, Brent's parents had a new Chevy station wagon. They kindly offered, "Take our car. We'll get along fine with the 'White Charger' for a couple of weeks."

So our honeymoon, which had consisted mostly of being Utah tour guides to my parents, now turned into a touring marathon. Tennessee is a long way from Utah and my home was in the eastern portion only a few miles short of North Carolina. Brent studied three major routes across America and we drove a route which appeared to be the most direct, but it was still an estimated 2,200 miles one way. That meant we would have to travel nearly 800 miles per day to make it in three days.

Now keep in mind that I had never been a fast driver nor a long distance driver. Also, remember that I never did anything life-threatening, that is, until I met and married Brent. I'd known Brent over a year and knew two things about him that should have warned me my life just might be full of adventure. First, working on his grandparents' ranch or on farms near his home in Washington, he had many times worked from dawn until midnight to herd cattle or sheep, milk cows, and get the hay in the barn before the next rainstorm. Clearly he could handle long hours. Second, Brent's high school mascot had been the Tolt Demons, and in driving long distances, he would certainly hold up to that name.

I still didn't fully see what was coming when he packed breakfasts, lunches and dinners, with corresponding drinks and snacks, in an ice chest the night before. The next morning it was still dark when he roused me to begin the marathon. Wisely, I took my pillow and favorite "blankie" and was still sleeping when we drove east into the rising sun somewhere in Colorado.

I could not sleep forever, though I learned it would have been an act of mercy. Finally I awoke to signs of hunger and bladder tension. I lovingly spoke to my handsome husband, "Good morning, Honey. I gotta go."

"Well good morning to you, Sunshine!" he responded. "You'll have to hold it a little longer, Babe, until we stop for gas. We can't afford to waste any time on unnecessary stops if we're going to make it to your folks place in three days. Now why don't you just cross your cute little legs and eat your breakfast. We've got a ways to go before this tank runs out. We're really makin' great time, Hon, but we gotta keep it up."

"Is he serious?" I thought to myself while sneaking a peek at the gas gage. *"This puppy still has a quarter tank. How long is that? Two hours or more? I'll never make it! I know I agreed to marry this man 'for better or for worse,' but bathroom breaks had better be included in that commitment."*

I fumed desperately in my mind as we raced toward Kansas at 80 miles per hour while I sat there with my legs crossed chewing on a bologna sandwich smothered in Miracle Whip for breakfast.

"I knew Brent was a frugal man when I married him. To think I actually admired that," I thought as I wiped Miracle Whip from my face. *"Like son, like father...of course his father bought a car that would go more miles between fill-ups than any like-size car on the planet. What am I to do? Here I sit next to a man I profess to love who is driving like a demon to set a transcontinental record, and only now do I learn he comes with a cast iron bladder."*

Well, somehow I survived that trip, undoubtedly with an immensely stretched bladder and greater endurance that I thought possible. On those rare occasions when we stopped, mostly just for gas of course, I learned to take full advantage. I went directly to the restroom, even if I had to fight another lady for the key. And then I ran around, did stretches and jumping jacks. We made it to Johnson City, Tennessee, in the allotted three days, having driven about sixteen hours per day.

We only had one major setback, Brent was pulled over for driving 82 miles per hour in a 75 mph zone. The officer would not allow us to proceed until he followed us into a little town where we were forced to pay the Justice of the Peace a $70 fine. Only then were we freed to go. When my dad heard about that, it was one of the few times I heard him swear, "D**** speed traps. That's how those little towns make extra money."

My parents' home was built into a hillside so you walked into the front door at ground level upstairs, but entered into the back door basement at ground level downstairs. The backyard with Dad's lush garden was about thirty feet lower than the front yard.

Brent and I had the downstairs apartment to ourselves. It included two bedrooms, a bath, and a small room with a kitchen that opened onto a cement patio overlooking the sloping garden and backyard. Brent had never been in the southern United States where the humidity is so high.

When we pulled back the covers for some much needed rest that first night, he said, "These sheets feel damp." And they remained that way—that night and every night.

"It's called mildew," I said. "Everything in Tennessee during the summer time is either wet or rusty."

The next evening was the open house and it was wonderful. Relatives, friends and neighbors I hadn't seen for over a year came to congratulate me and meet Brent. A couple of girl-cousins my same age whispered in my ear, "Wow, he's a hunk." Everybody who met Brent instantly liked him.

Brent shared with me three features that stood out to him; first the home had a tin roof that hummed a marvelously soothing sound when it rained. Second, the large, covered front porch that stretched across the front of the house was as homey as a front room, and during summer rains even more refreshing. We sat in couches and lounge chairs, visiting to a backdrop of rain sounds, be they the rhythmic melody of a cooling drizzle or the roar of a massive cloudburst prefaced by approaching thunder. The setting was as I imagined the eye of a tornado with nature's storm brewing all around, yet from the safety of that comforting old porch one remained bone dry.

The third unique feature was charming Poplar Street. Running north from the corner of our upper house, the street was so narrow as to be decreed "one way," with just enough space for resident cars to park on the east side, leaving a lane wide enough for moving cars to drive north. And what a quaint drive it was, lined on both sides with trees that reached out and tickled one another thirty feet up, creating for blocks an enchanting tree tunnel of Elms, Locusts, Poplars, and Maples. At lower heights were bursting white blooms of Dogwood declaring boldly their approval of summer.

Meanwhile, we visited the home where my father was born with the help of a country doctor. Like Poplar Street, his home was cut into a hillside, and isolated in the mountains on one of the Smokey Mountain ranges.

We went to see another uncle and his wife in their huge rock home. Built over one hundred years ago on Stoney Creek, it had been updated with modern heating, cooling, plumbing, and so on. We were fascinated by the spring house, a pioneer form of refrigeration. It consisted of a small stone building maybe eight feet by six feet, built on a flat rock where the cold creek water flowed thru a few inches high, cooling buckets of milk, cream, fruits, vegetables, and jugs of apple cider, or perhaps other favorite beverages of the day such as moonshine.

Brent played a tennis tournament at Milligan College and lost in the final to one of my former boyfriends. How that frustrated Brent. He wanted to be the best for his new bride and to show off for my girl cousins who insisted on coming. To us, winning or losing mattered little. We had no idea how to keep score. We just enjoyed watching the hunk.

Aunt Maude, widowed and retired, had been a very successful antique dealer. Her home in Elizabethton was like a small museum. Every nook and cranny was filled with rare and priceless objects, all tastefully arranged. Her aging body was frail, her mind sharp and her detailed descriptions of world travels in search of uncommon treasures most intriguing.

Some of our most comical ventures occurred at the farm of my grandparents Garland out on King Springs Road where we had lived before moving to the Poplar Street home. At the urging of family, Grandpa Garland took us to the back fence and demonstrated his singular cattle call. Within seconds dairy cattle emerged from the grove of trees at the top of the hill where they sheltered from the midday heat. They trotted down through the hillside pasture and came right up to Grandpa. You may never have suspected such a thing, but he loved his cows and they loved him.

Grandpa and the Lawnmower

Grandpa Garland tended toward shyness and normally said little, overshadowed by Grandma Garland who was quite a talker. But you know, Grandpa and Brent really took to one another and before we realized it, they silently slipped out onto the front porch for their own conversation. Between Grandma's strong voice echoing from the kitchen and Grandpa's thick southern drawl, Brent had difficulty understanding Grandpa initially. The eastern Tennessee dialect comes from the Welch that settled there hundreds of years ago.

Brent later said, "It was like being in a foreign country where I had studied the language just enough to recognize a word here and there. I missed most of what he said about his cows and years of farming. By the time he got to telling me about what it was like being in his seventies, I was getting on to his accent."

Here's an example of what Brent faced when talking with Grandpa.

"Brent, I'm a warnin' ya, ya'll don't wanna' git old. They's days when m' a'thritis 'n m' back aches sa' bad I cain't ev'n mow m' own lawn anymo'. But a few week back, I had me the dangdest experience. M' lawnmowe' wudn't start so I got out m' tools 'n began tinkerin' with it. I cleaned th' carbeerator 'n made adjustments 'n poured in oil and gas ev'rywhere. I wa'rshed 'd air filter wit gas and put ev'rything back togethe' and dat old mower ran like a Caddeelac. But what's mo' seeprizin', so did I! I mowed m' whole lawn in less'n an hour. It was like I's forty agin. I ain't felt s' good in years. I was still feelin' good when I laid me down fer the night. But then came the mornin'. When I waked, I cud hardly move. There weren't a spot on m' body that didn't ache. I thot, 'What the heck is a goin' on? Yeste'day ya'll felt s' good . . . like a new man.' And then it hit me—it was the gas! I'd worked on that mower nigh onto an hour with all them gas fumes risin' up into m' face the whole time. I'd had me a gasoline high. That's what made me feel real good. But now I was payin' fer it. 'Spite o' the pain, I had me a good laf over that one. Yes siree, I did."

The Honeymoon Ends

As they say, "All good things must end." So it was with our Tennessee honeymoon. Bright and early came the morning in which we said our good-byes through tears of gratitude, hugs, "I love you" and "Drive safely." The last few days in Tennessee I began to feel ill. I did not realize it then, but it may have been early signs of "morning sickness." What a blessing it was that Brent's parents had loaned us their roomy station wagon.

Brent was most considerate of my condition. He folded down the back seats and stacked our wedding "loot" carefully to one side so he could make me a narrow but full-length bed on the other. That bed, well padded with blankets, sleeping bags and a pillow, became my main accommodation on the trip home since I was not well enough to sit up for very long.

For the next three days Brent was two different kinds of people. First, he was my kind nursemaid, doing all he could to make me comfortable. But when he got behind the wheel, he again became my demon driver. When he hit the freeway heading west he shot right up to 80 miles per hour, hesitant to go any faster due to the speeding ticket he'd received coming east. It was quite a sensation to lie in the back of the car watching clouds rush by and thinking, "This must be what it feels like to ride in a rocket."

Up front, my Demon Race Driver sat hunched forward vigilantly with a vice-like grip on the steering wheel. Meanwhile, he kept his lead foot on the gas pedal. On the seat next to him was a large box filled with at least three days worth of sandwiches, snacks and drinks.

In back, when I would awaken from the relief of sleep and again feel the pain, I would often let a moan escape my lips. Brent would ask, "How're ya' doin?" He'd picked up a little southern drawl of his own. "Ya'll need a rest stop?"

I was grateful for his consideration, and he was gracious to offer me more rest stops. Additional delays came when we got into some construction where for many miles of dirt and gravel road. We were often limited to a measly 40 miles per hour. As a result, on the third day Brent was determined to get us home where I could get proper rest and care, so he drove more than twenty hours straight. We arrived at our USU apartment after 4 a.m. The honeymoon was over!

I went to the doctor for fatigue and nausea, and after a few tests, I found out that I was pregnant. For a girl whom the doctor said would probably never be able to have children, I couldn't help but wonder—how did this happen?

I had moved into my husband's bachelor apartment and we turned two twin beds into one king size bed. We were only a few nights home from our honeymoon, but I was already praying at the side of that make-shift bed that I could have a baby. I had always wanted to have a baby, so much that I could never really image myself doing anything else.

A baby! Me and Brent! Wow, this baby would be beautiful. This baby would be the most amazing child in the world. I couldn't stop thinking about it. A little life was growing inside me and it was a dream come true. I drove home, not really knowing how I would tell Brent.

Is this what he wanted? So soon? But I already knew he wanted what I wanted. I pulled into the parking lot and walked downstairs to our basement apartment.

"Honey, we're having a baby," I said as he came home that night.

With a twinkle in his eye (why does he always have that twinkle in his eye?), he said, "I warned ya!"

Within days of being told I was pregnant, I went to the thrift store and purchased a baby doll dress. It was loose in the tummy and even though my stomach was as flat as a board, I still felt I wanted my baby to have room to roam. I went to visit the Bunnells and walked into their house with my maternity-looking dress on.

"Guess what, I'm pregnant." They were a bit shocked, but I didn't care. I was having a baby!

Pregnancy and Ding Dongs

Brent was back in his doctoral classes and I was still recovering from the drive across the country.

I decided that couple-time together to adjust to married life before launching into parenthood was probably overrated. I was not even sure I could have children and here I was, already expecting a baby.

We've all heard stories of weird appetites and bizarre emotions in pregnant women. Well, I could have become the poster child.

I burst into tears over things like a dog food commercial for Gravy Train. Watching that little dog round the corner, bursting into the doggy door and into the arms of his owner was just a bit too much. For days at a time all I could eat was orange popsicles and only a half at a time. When Brent wanted to go for a run or play tennis with a friend after classes, it was fine with me. The very smell of him that I loved so much before could now bring on nausea or even a fit of throwing up. All the while, Brent was striving to be patient and make my life easier.

He became concerned about my inability to eat, or if I did, my inability to keep it down. He constantly searched for foods that did not make me nauseous at their sight or smell. He did most of the food shopping because I couldn't handle the smells in a grocery store. Still in college, our money was limited so we shopped frugally. One day he stopped by the day-old bread store. On that day the special was Ding Dongs, chocolate frosted cupcakes with whipped cream centers. Yum! They were one of our favorites and he could not resist.

Brent returned to our apartment with a bag containing a very healthy loaf of whole wheat bread for half-price, and two less healthy Ding Dongs. A pregnant woman's sense of smell is truly supernatural. Brent was still clear across the room when I rolled over on the coach and looked at him, "Umm, that smells good. What are you eating?"

"Chocolate Ding Dongs," he said, holding one out to me.

I snatched that Ding Dong, tore off the wrapper, scarfed it down in seconds and sat there licking my lips. "Do you have any more?" He gave me the other Ding Dong and I quickly took care of it the same way. I was thrilled. I hadn't eaten like this in days. Brent and I waited, but five, then ten minutes passed and I showed no sign of dashing for the bathroom.

"Babe, I'll be right back," Brent announced. He ran out of our apartment, leaped into the *White Charger*, and tore back down the hill to the day-old bread store where he bought twenty more Ding Dongs for a dollar. He drove back up the hill to our apartment with the bag full of twenty Ding Dongs to save me and our future child from starvation.

"More Ding Dongs, just like you asked," he said, catching his breath from the long flight of stairs he'd just ran down.

I stared down into that mass of twenty Ding Dongs. Suddenly they began to spin before my eyes, like a chocolate cesspool. I sprinted to the bathroom just in time.

I eventually staggered from the bathroom, pale and visibly shaken. "Keep those things out of my sight," I ordered.

Coleslaw...Please, Please!

After the Ding Dong dilemma, my main goal in life became pondering about various foods and then considering if I could tolerate them. Brent had been attentive, doing his best to prepare meals or dart out to find any little whim expressed. The problem was the rules kept changing. A food that appealed to me this minute might bring on a scurry for the bathroom five minutes later. Not only was this cycle causing me an energy low, but I was especially concerned about providing adequate nutrition to the baby. Having nausea as a constant companion was challenging. Even when the symptoms left, it was temporary and then they returned with a vengeance. The search for foods went on. Then one day I became very excited. I had a craving for coleslaw!

Now we know that no one makes better (or more) coleslaw than Colonel Sanders, the master of "Kentucky Fried." Unfortunately, the Colonel, who could have easily saved the day, had not yet found residence in the mountain town of Logan, Utah. Brent always ready, pledged to bring in the coleslaw if he had to go to every restaurant in town— all three of them. After two failed attempts, he approached the last café. "Please, please, Lord, let there be coleslaw at The Lofthouse," he thought.

Brent entered The Lofthouse and asked desperately, "Do you have coleslaw?"

"Sorry sir, it's Thursday and we only serve coleslaw on Tuesday.

We have several other excellent salads."

Brent was running out of options. "I can't wait until next Tuesday. My wife is pregnant and for days has eaten nothing but popsicles, only the orange ones."

The waitress looked a little puzzled by, restated the facts. "I'm really sorry sir; we just don't have any coleslaw on Thursdays. You'll have to try somewhere else."

Then Brent peeked his head around the counter into "Employees Only" territory and saw a chef in a white apron working in the kitchen. Here was his last option.

"Can you please make me some coleslaw for my pregnant wife?"

To my relief and in an act of mercy, she did!

Within twenty minutes, Brent was riding hard to the rescue in the *White Charger* packing a full pint of the lifesaving prescription. Again he'd saved me and our child, this time with coleslaw. He walked into our apartment and my eyes lit up like an eagle after a rabbit. And the best part of the story is I actually kept it down!

A Daughter

Nine months and 14 days after our wedding, I realized I was in labor. Brent had bought a rocking chair for me and put it in our bedroom. I was up in the middle of the night rocking away. I waited for a while, hoping the contractions would go away. I was afraid. Would I really have to go through labor? I remembered old English gothic novels where women gave birth in the bell tower and the screams of her pain could be heard around the city. I hadn't really bothered to educate myself on delivery, so I wasn't sure what a modern-day woman should expect.

The contractions were getting unbearable, so I packed my suitcase and woke Brent up. He was perfectly calm, always the professional and we drove the speed limit to the hospital, stopping at every red light and every stop sign. We checked into the hospital and I was assigned a room, but when the doctor came in, he didn't want Brent to stay with me.

"Brent, this may take a while, so why don't you go home and I'll give you a call when things progress," the doctor said.

So Brent kissed me goodbye and left. If I was frightened before, I was really frightened now.

A nurse insisted the bed lay flat and instructed me to lay on my back. I was so uncomfortable, but I did as I was told. She left and I started crying. When the shift changed, a new nurse came in.

"What are you doing on your back?" She propped up the bed and helped me roll over to my side. I was much more comfortable, but still scared. The doctor came in and broke my water and I wasn't sure what was happening. I didn't know the pain I was feeling was my body's natural way of pushing a baby out. . . . and the pain was getting more and more intense. They wheeled me into the delivery room and I started crying for my mom. The pain and the fear were more then I could bear when the nurse put a mask over my face. When I woke up, I was a mother.

My perfect baby daughter was lying in the hospital bassinet, wrapped up like an Eskimo. She squinted her eyes under the bright lights and I asked if I could hold her. In my arms, she finally opened her eyes and I caught a glimpse of heaven.

During my pregnancy, Brent read dozens of baby books, scouring for the perfect name. We agreed on the name Krista, which means "little follower of the Lord."

"I'd like for her to have your middle name," he insisted. Elaine means light.

It was a perfect name for our little princess.

When Krista was a baby, we moved to Wyoming where Brent worked as a director of the counseling department for a small private college. We lived in a home on campus and I was the girl's dorm-mother.

One evening while holding my infant daughter in my arms, I marveled at her perfect little features, her lips, her fingernails—the way her hair swirled on the top of her head. To be a mother was more than I had ever dreamed of. Krista shared the same features as her daddy, including dark brown eyes that made me melt. She looked up at me with such love.

I reflected on the night Brent had prayed, thanking God for bringing us together, and when I had heard the choir of angels singing. The wonder of holding my daughter, my own child straight from heaven filled me with a love only God could understand.

Knowledge was given to me then during that sacred moment with my new baby. Within the choir of angels I had heard that night was our unborn children, even this beautiful baby I was holding. Before Krista was born, she knew I was her mother. She knew her daddy. She was destined to be ours and God knew it. In reflection, this was my first prebirth experience.

Little did I know that there would be many more visits with these angels, our future children waiting to come to our family.

Mother and I at our home on King Springs Road in Johnson City, Tennessee, 1949.

My grandmother Naoma Garland Street in 1921 with my dad on her lap. I have felt Grandmother Naoma with me on several occasions throughout my life.

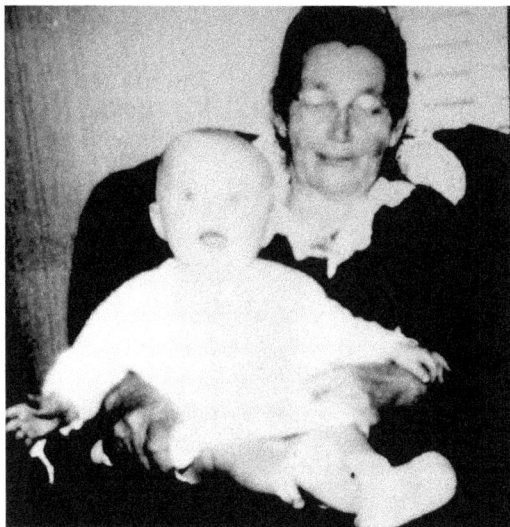

That is me sitting on the lap of my grandmother I was named after, Sarah Whitson Garland. She was the snuff chewing, Bible-reading great-grandmother whom I loved so much.

Here I am at age 5. I have always loved animals and nature.

With my cousin Mike on one of the few horses I have ever sat on. Notice the frightened look on my face!

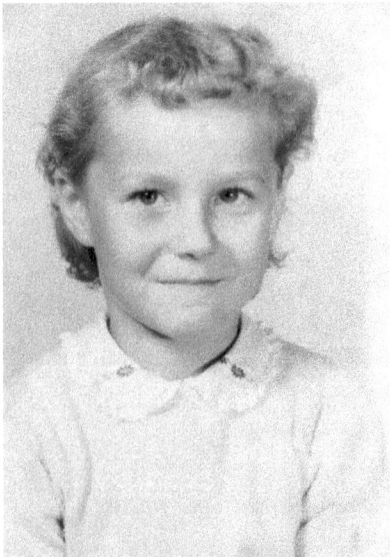

My 1st grade picture in 1953. I was five years old when I spontaneously left my body in search of God.

In my daddy's arms, where I always felt safe and loved.

Ready for church on Easter morning with my beautiful sister Sandra. Mother wore hats and gloves to church and I always admired her elegance.

April 1970. Sneaking a hug with Brent during our engagement photos in Logan Canyon, Utah, We were married on June 3, 1970 in Salt Lake City, Utah.

My 24 inch waist vanished after my first child was born.

Steve and Helen Bunnell, at their home in Brigham City, Utah in 1968. They are eternal friends, who taught me I was a child of God.

Proud as punch during my first pregnancy, Christmas 1970.

A year after our wedding in 1971, I held our brand new baby, Krista. I was in awe that I had a child after my doctor told me that I would probably never be able to have children.

PART II

FINDING ANSWERS

A Birthday Message

Before Krista's first birthday, I received heartbreaking news. My dear friend, Helen Bunnell, had passed away. She was only 61. She had been like a mother to me, taking me into her home, making meals for me, placing fresh flowers by my bedside from time to time. I would never forget her strong Christian faith, her cheerfulness and her pristine intellect. From the time I met her, she encouraged me that I would find my mission in life. Now, I would have to carry on without her.

In the short time I'd known Helen, she had made my birthdays special by making and decorating a homemade cake and buying thoughtful gifts, wrapped and tied with ribbons. On my birthday the first year after her death, she appeared to me in a dream. I have learned that birthdays have significance for those in heaven as well as on earth and that loved ones who have passed over may be with us on our birthday or theirs.

In this dream I was back in the Bunnells' home in Brigham City. Steve Bunnell was in the living room reading in his favorite rocking chair. Helen walked through the kitchen door into the living room to greet me. She was dressed in white, beautiful and younger than when she had died. She was not wearing her glasses—apparently they're not needed in heaven!

Helen took my hand and walked me into the kitchen. There was a sheer white curtain there and, still holding my hand, she walked me through it into the spirit world. There is a dimension of heaven right here on earth, but our natural eyes can't see it, neither can our natural ears hear it, but when allowed, we are given glimpses that heaven is all around us.

In that world of angels, hand in hand with Helen, we began flying through a daytime sky over endless wheat fields. "The field is ripe and ready to harvest," she said, pointing below.

I had floods of knowledge given to me. There with her, I remembered what I had known before I was born. I tried to retain the knowledge, but most of it left me upon awaking. But one thing I remembered clearly—she told me I had a mission in which I would someday write about the heavenly world we come from before we are born.

What did that mean? I had never aspired to be a writer. I had never written anything of any significance before. I was busy with my daughter and taking care of our home. I was puzzled by Helen's message for a number of years before I learned just what the dream meant and what kind of writing would be required of me to fulfill that part of my mission here on the earth.

Krista's Healing

In January 1972, Brent accepted a college teaching position in southern California. The moving van took awhile to arrive with our belongings and we were living in a motel with no kitchen. The long drive from Wyoming had been hard on our first child, Krista. She was ten months old and for several days manifested symptoms of dysentery, throwing up or losing to diarrhea all her liquids and food. Without a kitchen available, it was diffcult to prepare mild warm baby meals.

We were worried about Krista suffering from dehydration, but California was in the middle of a rash of malpractice suits against doctors. No doctor would see Krista for fear we were gold-diggers, seeking to sue.

For eight days we prayed daily for our daughter. We were feeding her with an eye-dropper, and even those tiny amounts caused her to throw up. She was failing. At last we met a church member who referred us to a doctor, assuring him that we would not sue. The doctor examined Krista briefly and immediately arranged for us to take her to the hospital.

We rushed to the Burbank Hospital and Krista was admitted. She was in the final stages of dehydration . . . her skin was flaking off. After several painful tries the doctor concluded that Krista's blood vessels were too small to receive a needle for intravenous fluids. He chose the alternative of inserting large needles of an intravenous drip into the thick muscles of her thighs and hoping the liquids would absorb into her body rapidly enough to reverse the dehydration.

The hospital crib had metal bars. We peered through those bars—like prison bars—at our daughter, needles protruding from her thighs, Her skin was chalky pale, cracking and flaking. Her eyes were sunken into her skull. Those eyes were normally bright and smiling, but now they were glazed over and remote. Our robust child was shrunken . . . tiny. We spoke to her but she didn't recognize us.

In her precarious condition, the doctor advised us to leave our daughter and go get some rest before we also became ill. We dragged ourselves back to the motel, tried to eat a little snack, prayed for our daughter and then fell exhausted into bed into a fitful sleep.

We awakened early. Where were we? Oh yes, we are in California and our daughter is in the hospital. It is Saturday. We shower, eat, pray and drive to the hospital. We peered through the bars at our daughter. There was little change. We are still unrecognized. We stayed by her side for the day, praying, hoping.

We learned that the next day, Sunday, a conference of our church is being held in Burbank. The visiting speaker is Apostle Howard W. Hunter, a former resident of Pasadena to the southeast of Burbank. We believe in miracles. We have prayed for, fasted for, and laid on hands and blessed our child in the name of Jesus, but sometime additional faith is needed. We had read where modern apostles, men of great faith who, when they could not go in person, sent an object such as a handkerchief with another to bless and heal the sick.

On Sunday morning we determined to fast yet again time for our daughter. Brent attended the church conference. Howard W. Hunter was the concluding speaker. The choir sang the closing hymn and the closing prayer was offered. As the congregation filed out, Brent approached Apostle Hunter on the stand, introduced himself and explained the situation with our daughter. Brent withdrew from his suit pocket a clean white handkerchief and one of Krista's small pink corduroy booties. He then asked, "Brother Hunter, will you please hold these objects in your hand, add your faith to ours, and then authorize me to take the objects to the hospital and bless our child?"

Brother Hunter reached forward and shook Brent's hand with the objects in between their hands. He stood that way a few seconds as he stared into the distance as though listening for something. Finally he looked with tear-filled eyes into Brent's eyes and said with authority, "Now brother, go heal your daughter in the name of Jesus Christ!"

Brent thanked him and stepped down from the stand with those blessed objects in his hand. He met me at the hospital around noon where Krista still did not recognize us. We knelt by the crib and Brent reached through the metal bars, gently laying the clean white handkerchief and the pink corduroy bootie on Krista's head before blessing her to be made whole in the name of Jesus Christ. Two days later she was discharged from the hospital. Our smiling, vibrant Krista was back.

Are Angels Watching?

In California we were blessed with two more children. Laura Lynn came first, followed by our first son, Rodney Brent. With young children, it was a thrill to be 40 minutes from Disneyland and 30 minutes from the beach, but my health did not agree with the pollution of Los Angeles. I was hospitalized twice with severe breathing problems. Doctors said my condition was life- threatening and getting worse. The cure required moving to a place with cleaner air.

We didn't want to move. Brent loved serving as lay Bishop of our congregation and he liked his teaching job. We gave up a lot, but decided to move back to the cleaner air of Utah for my health and so that Krista could begin kindergarten there. We moved into a hillside home with a terrific view, kitty-corner from Brent's Aunt June and Uncle Dee, and a mile from his parents.

It was fun to decorate each child's room. For a special outing, I took three-year-old Rod to the store. He picked out wallpaper with scenes of horses. He loved playing cowboys and Indians, so this was just what he wanted. The carpet we picked out for his bedroom was green, pasture-like next to the western scene of the wallpaper. The wallpaper had been hung earlier in the day and I made the finishing touches, spreading out a homemade tie quilt on his bed. His room was perfect.

I had dinner to get ready, so I left Rod in his room. I was in the kitchen when Rod came running down the hall. He called out, "Mommy, Mommy, come look at my room."

He was insistent there was something important for me to see, so I put down my cooking spoon and down the hallway we went. I walked into his bedroom and saw the artwork of my child, drawn with a black permanent magic marker all over the new wallpaper.

I paused in a moment of reflection, knowing very well I could react with anger. I was angry and disappointed. The room was ruined. I wanted to punish him for his actions, when I felt a presence behind me.

"Don't you dare spank that child, just teach him right from wrong," a voice came clearly into my mind. I knew it was my Grandma Naoma. Her voice was so clear that I turned around expecting to see her. Grandmother Naoma had died when my dad was five years old, so I had never met her, but from time to time I have felt her near me.

I looked at my son. He loved what he had done. This was his room. It was his badge of honor. With a different perspective, I could live with the marker on my wall. After I praised his artwork and making sure my anger was under control, I taught Rod he should always ask before drawing on a wall. He promised he would. Oh, and I made a mental note to hide all permanent magic markers that were in my house.

As I left Rod's "doubly decorated" room, a thought entered my mind. "How often am I watched by angels when I don't even know they are there?"

It made me realize my life wasn't just mine. I was on sacred duty caring for my children. Unseen eyes were upon me at all times and it was my duty to honor my role as mother.

Mothering 101

Our second son, Tadd, was born later that year. I had my first four children in six years.

Four little ones to care for, nurture, and love. There were dishes to wash, always the dishes. I cooked most of my meals from scratch. I had several things I tried to do each day—clean bodies, clean clothes, healthy food, loving words, loving touch, prayer and reading time. Some days I did better than others.

God sends each child with a unique personality and unique needs. Some children are sensitive, others are comedians. Sometimes they are both at once. But whenever possible, they always need love from both their mother and father.

Someone once said, "God could not be everywhere, so He made mothers." When children are small they love positive time with their parents. They love beautiful music, classical or hymns. When I was a child, some of my happiest times were when my mother would sit down and read to me or make a doll dress by hand.

Children need to be held and touched in gentle ways to make them feel loved. Sometimes we give birth to children, but then get too busy to rear them properly with love and attention.

My mother taught me about prayer when I was very little. I learned some things at church, but it was mainly my mother who taught me about God through her personal stories of faith and miracles. She loved the scriptures and had great faith in the power of prayer. Many times I sat on the floor nearby and watched her kneel at her bed and pray.

I listened to her words, simple words, but it was like God was sitting on the other side of the bed watching and listening to every word she spoke.

When I was around three years old, Mother injured her foot. She wrapped it in gauze and taped it with white tape. There was a large sore under the white gauze when she took it off for her bath. One day she was very discouraged about the pain and discomfort.

I asked, "Mommy, can I pray for your leg? Jesus will help it get all better."

She said, "Yes, you pray."

I prayed a simple child's prayer and within a few days the sore was all gone—Jesus had heard and answered my prayer.

I learned as a little child that miracles are possible. It took faith in God, but God is a God of miracles.

A Prayer for Patience

One day when our son Tadd was little I went to my room, knelt by my bed, and asked the Lord to give me patience. I needed patience with myself—I realized that I could not do it all. I had to cut myself some slack, I could not keep a perfectly clean house, and always look like I just stepped out of a fashion magazine.

Tadd knelt by me and listened to that prayer. He smiled when we were done, his big brown eyes watching me. I told him I loved being his mommy and he was a special child of God. A feeling entered my heart and I knew I was on God's errand. I knew that some things were of greater importance than a perfectly clean house. Every act of love I shared with my children was my way of praising God.

Over time, I gave myself permission to not worry about trying to do it all. I learned to choose peace, and dismiss anxiety about having a perfect house all the time. I learned that I could sit down on top of a pile of laundry and not be bothered about it. For years, I had a huge sock box. The kids would go through it if they needed socks, and I still think wearing matching socks is overrated. If they are at least the same color, it works!

Me, a Writer?

In the midst of the constant activity that goes on in a large family, I periodically had promptings about writing, but it seemed ridiculous because there was no time. It was strange to think that anyone as busy as I just barely surviving could have the emotional energy to create.

I felt deep in my heart that I had something to share, a work to do, but with the inspiration came discouragement too. "Who do you think you are?" a voice would say. "You're not a writer, so don't even attempt to do this. You will fail miserably if you do."

One Sunday I was praying—seeking answers that only God could provide. We had attended church in the morning and that afternoon I was enjoying a rare and much appreciated time of peace and quiet while the little children napped and the older children were busy with their activities. The phone rang. It was my friend Denise. In her quiet time that day, she had taken a nap and was excited to tell me about a dream she'd had about me. In fact, she wanted to come over right then. Curious, of course I said, "Come on over."

Soon Denise entered through the patio door and we shared a hug. I was happy to see her and most anxious to hear her dream. We sat down on the living room couch and she began. "I was napping today after dinner and had a very vivid dream about you," she said. "I saw you in heaven before you were born. You were visiting with Heavenly Father and Jesus about what you would do here on earth. Heavenly Father placed His hands gently on your head and gave you a blessing. I heard part of this blessing and I am here to tell you about it."

I listened intently as she added, "He said, 'You will write books about unborn children. Through your books the children preparing for birth will have a voice, and you will be their advocate. Your books will touch hearts that are indifferent toward children and parenting. Your books will help multitudes of unborn children come to earth who otherwise would be blocked or rejected.'"

"What do you think it means?" I asked her. "How could anyone write about children coming from heaven to earth?"

"I don't know," Denise responded. "But when it is time, the Lord will teach you, of that I am certain."

For days I pondered and prayed about Denise's dream. At last I received my own confirmation that it was true, but I was still unclear how to proceed.

Meanwhile, I continued caring for our family and Brent worked hard to provide for us. It was a period of faith strengthening. I continued to ponder the impressions to write, all the while praying for answers of how to accomplish what I feared was an impossible mission. How could I ever fulfill such a task? Only through God, I assured myself.

I knew all too well that I was one of the "weak things" of the earth. But I also knew that God often uses the "weak things" of the earth to do His work here.

Time to Write

One evening Brent took me to listen to a popular Christian author speak about his books. He spoke with great passion and shared the idea that each of us have a unique mission all our own, and that if we have faith in Christ He will help us accomplish what we need to do. While the author was speaking, I saw a beam of light to his right. I realized the light was shaped in the outline of a person. I asked Brent it he saw it. "Yes," he said.

We listened with greater intent to the message of the author, knowing he spoke things of truth.

The next day, I awoke with a message in my mind: "Today, you need to write."

I knelt in prayer, asking, "God, what should I write?" The image of a woman from church came into my mind. This woman, Laura, (another Laura, not my daughter) was disabled and mentally challenged and lived with her mother. I was blessed with the church assignment to visit them monthly with friendship, encouragement and to check on their needs. That morning I envisioned a human- interest story I could write about, my experience with Laura.

This is how it turned out:

I was busy running errands one Saturday afternoon when I drove by Laura's home. I decided to make a surprise visit. I pulled into the driveway of her mother's humble little home and knocked on the door. The widowed mother invited me in and quickly excused herself back into the kitchen where she was cooking.

There was Laura.

She was timid and rarely came out of her room during my visits but today she was sitting in a rocking chair with one leg propped on a footstool. At first she seemed startled by my presence, but after I stooped down and inquired about her injured foot, she was calmed.

I felt the Holy Spirit prompt me in a quiet, humbling way, and as thoughts came to my mind, I spoke them to Laura. "I wish you could join us at church, it would be special for all of us to know you better and enjoy your sweet spirit."

"I'd come, but I have a large growth on my foot. I have hardly been able to wear shoes for months, and it really hurts when I try to walk."

I looked at her foot again. Yes, there was a large growth. I could see it now, and I could see the difficulty of her going anywhere that required walking.

Then came this thought from the Spirit, "Her foot problem is now your problem. What are you going to do about it?"

"Should I take her to the doctor?" I thought, and the Spirit urged, "Yes, now."

"This moment?" I questioned, startled. "Yes," the voice spoke to my mind.

Well, here goes. "Laura, can I help you with your foot? My husband's Uncle Dee is a doctor. He's off today and he lives across the street from our house. Will you go with me to his home so we can ask him if he can help you?"

Laura looked fearful for a moment, then relaxed and said, "Yes, if you'll help me get ready."

I helped her up and she leaned on me to walk-hop into her room, a touchingly simple room. How many hours—how many years—had Laura sat on that bed, alone with her thoughts and feelings? As I stood in the doorway watching her gather some things together, I was blessed with the power of the Holy Ghost more powerfully than before. I felt as if the Master was standing by. Tears came to my eyes. The Lord was truly aware of this humble woman, Laura, and her needs. I was His servant to help her. His teachings entered my mind, simple, yet powerful, "Feed my sheep." He had also said, "Love one another." (John 13:34)

I explained my intent to Laura's mother. She was grateful someone would take such an interest in her daughter. She had thought the growth an inalterable result of the polio Laura suffered when she was thirteen.

I helped Laura to my car and we drove to Uncle Dee's home. Dr. Dee Cutler was one of those doctors who would always help those in pain whether they could pay or not.

He graciously invited us in and kindly examined Laura's foot. She had suffered this ailment over half of her life and had been unable to walk correctly or without pain since her bout with polio. Poverty and fear had prevented her from seeking medical help.

Uncle Dee felt the ailment was correctable and arranged for Laura to see a foot specialist in his clinic within a few days.

After the specialist examined Laura's foot, he came to the waiting room and asked, "Are you Laura's sister?"

"Well, I'm her sister in the church," I said.

He smiled, understanding. "She told me to come and talk to her sister who was waiting for her. She needs immediate surgery," he continued. "After that, Laura should walk almost perfectly for the first time in twenty-five years."

"That's wonderful, but I don't know if they can pay."

"Dr. Cutler mentioned that," he said. "If there's any problem with finances, I'll gladly do the surgery free." He smiled again and I knew the Spirit of God was with us.

Shortly after the exam, Laura had the surgery. Everything went well. I went to see her the next day in the hospital. Laura looked radiant. She was actually up and walking gently but correctly, thrilled at the prospect of normal mobility. Her foot healed rapidly. Before long all the bandages were off and she was free to go anywhere she wanted.

By this time I was making almost weekly trips to Laura's home to check on her progress. One morning as I was talking with her, the Spirit came again. My job was not done, "Now that her foot is better and she is able to walk properly, you need to help her f i nd something meaningful to do with her time."

I was not surprised, but nearly overcome with the realization, as never before, how much the Lord loves us and desires that we serve and care for one another.

I talked with Laura's mother about possible opportunities for schooling and work. She was cautiously excited. Laura had been housebound a long time. If she could do some things on her own, it would be a great blessing to both mother and daughter.

My husband had done some work with agencies that help the impaired. There was a special school for the handicapped in a nearby community.

Brent referred us to a friend there who arranged an appointment for Laura and me at the school.

When I picked up Laura that afternoon, her mother had bought her a new outfit. The clothes were simple and humble, but Laura looked beautiful. She was also nervous. This was a special day for her, a day of new adventure. She wasn't sure she could cope with school, yet she wanted with all her heart to succeed.

The school administrators treated Laura like royalty. She was thrilled as they escorted us around the school and told us about their two-part program: classes for part of the day and a sheltered work opportunity the other. Laura would actually earn money! Something beyond her furthest dreams just a few months earlier.

As we sat at the desk to fill out the papers, the director said, "Mrs. Hinze, we are excited that Laura can join us here at our school. May I take your name and address to keep you informed of her progress? However, I don't know what to call you on the form—friend? supporter? advocate? Yes, I think I'll call you advocate. Laura's advocate. How does that sound to you?"

Tears filled my eyes. "Advocate would be just fine."

With an old electric typewriter and while nursing my newest little daughter, Becky, I typed out the story as best as I could. I prayerfully went over and over it. It was the Lord's story and I wanted it to be just right. I was impressed to place the following scripture at the top of the page.

I am come that they might have life, and that they might have it more abundantly. (John 10:10)

Finally, it felt finished. I inserted the manuscript into an envelope and mailed it to a church magazine, *The Ensign*, and later that year, it was published. My writing career had begun.

Another Widow to Write About

After my article "Laura's Advocate" was published, the magazine editor asked if I would submit other ideas I had for additional articles.

At the request of two foster daughters who were living with us at the time, we listened to a tape of Matthew Cowley called *Miracles*. Matthew Cowley was a beloved leader in the LDS Church who, through great faith in the Lord, had the gift of healing with which he blessed many people. It was a sad day when he died unexpectedly of a heart attack at age 56 in the 1950s. Touched by the message on the tape, one foster daughter, Karen, asked to know more about this man. I mentioned this to a friend who casually commented, "I know Matthew Cowley's wife, Elva."

The coincidence should have struck me as odd, but I already knew of the mysterious workings of the Lord. I had no idea Matthew Cowley's widow was still living. My friend, with her five young kids, and me with my five, invited Elva, now 80 years old, to our home for Sunday dinner.

We developed a sweet friendship and Elva was most kind to our young daughter, Laura, who spent the evening asking all sorts of questions about Matthew. I, too, enjoyed the conversation. It was like I'd known Elva all my life. In this short time, I already felt a love for her like I felt for my own mother. When she left that evening, I said to Elva, "My mother is in Tennessee and I only see her once a year. You remind me so much of her."

In her sweet voice, Elva said, "Sarah, your mother must be very special, but if you need a mother in town, I'll be your mother."

A week later, I was driving downtown to see Elva when I felt someone near me in the car. I knew it was a man. A strong impression came into my mind—"Turn left down the next street where you will see a flower store. Go inside and buy Elva a bouquet of white camellias."

I was not up on my camellias, but surely the shop proprietor was. He arranged a bouquet of white flowers in full bloom with hundreds of petals and a sweet perfume-like fragrance. I carried the bouquet out to my car and continued the drive to Elva's apartment. The unseen man's presence in the car remained strong.

I arrived and rang the apartment doorbell. Elva opened the door and I handed her the bouquet. "These flowers are for you."

Her eyes got big and she burst into a smile. "Sarah, how did you know Matthew gave me white camellias?"

In her apartment that day my prayers were answered—my next

article was to be the story of Elva's life and the ministry she shared with her husband.

After much research and many interviews with Elva and friends who knew her, I submitted the story to the magazine. They were pleased with the article and accepted it for publication on the condition they could take a current photo of Elva. When I passed this request on to Elva, she gave a very feminine response, saying, "I have nothing to wear."

She went on to explain that Matthew took great pleasure in picking out and surprising her with new clothes. Elva said, "Matthew has been gone thirty years and I have nothing new to wear." I wasn't sure what to say.

A few days later I was in a shopping mall when I felt walking at my side—the same male presence I'd felt in the car. The impression came, "Buy Elva a new dress." By now I was certain this unseen friend was Elva's beloved husband, Matthew.

I didn't know Elva's size, only that she was petite. Being 5'10", I had never stepped into the petite section of a department store, and if I did, towering above the racks of clothing, people surely would think I was lost. Then if I tried to explain I was there being guided by a deceased husband to buy a dress for his petite 80-year-old widow, people would think I was not only lost, but loony!

Nevertheless, I entered unknown territory under the direction of my unseen helper whom I trusted would guide me to the right dress for his cherished wife. The racks were full of tiny little dresses that made me feel I'd entered a dollhouse. I browsed and browsed until I spotted a lilac-colored dress with a jacket and I sensed it was the one.

"What size?" I asked in my mind, knowing all too well not to speak out loud to an angel when he stands next to you at the mall. The impression came in my mind, "Size 5. That is the one."

I smiled. First camellia flowers, white of course, and now a lilac-colored dress! Elva would be pleased, knowing the love and concern of her husband for her welfare and happiness was not just of this world. Satisfied, I bought the dress.

Later, when Elva tried on the dress it fit just right and was a perfect accessory to her dark hair. When the photographer came for the photo shoot, I stood back and marveled at what heaven had done for Elva. A new bouquet of white camellias was on the table next to her, and she looked like the queen she was as she wore Matthew's gift to her.

My second article was also a success, but for reasons known only in heaven, it would be a while before I would be published again.

A Home with a Downstairs Apartment

When Tadd was three years old, I read a newspaper article about refugees from Cambodia and Laos. These countries near Vietnam were in the process of a communist coup.

People were fleeing for their lives due to civil war and genocide— the government was killing its own people. The Catholic, Mormon and other churches arranged programs to bring these refugees to safety in other countries, including the United States.

When Brent came home that night, I showed him the article and asked, "Can we sponsor a refugee family?"

"Let's pray about it." he responded.

After prayer he said, "Let's look into it and if we do it, I think we should ask for a family with children so our children can experience this with us too."

This is some amazing man. Brent has always been the first to help others in need, especially the underdog. We already had two foster daughters living with us. And a few months earlier the husband of a couple Brent was counseling went into a rage and literally threw his wife and six children out on the street.

Brent brought them to our home where they stayed for ten days until they could find a place of their own. The husband in that case was a hunter and threatened Brent with a rifle for "sticking his nose into my family business!"

Where will we put a refugee family? Every bedroom is full of our children and the foster daughters. But I knew God would provide.

The next week, a man who was referred to us by a mutual friend, came to our home with an interesting proposition. He had a large house that he wanted to trade for a smaller one, specifically our smaller house. We would have to borrow $30,000 extra for his larger house with a bigger lot and a downstairs two-bedroom apartment.

Up until this point, Brent and I had never considered leaving our quaint four-bedroom home near Aunt June and Uncle Dee, but we went over our finances and agreed it was a good move for our growing family, and our soon to be refugee family.

The deal was made and we moved into our new home a few weeks before we were assigned, at our request, a refugee family of 8 from Laos. The day before they arrived, I shopped at three different grocery stores. Assuming Laos to be a tropical climate, I brought home gallons of pineapple juice, every can of fish I could find and varieties of rice. I filled the shelves in the kitchen of our downstairs apartment.

The two bedrooms had been furnished with several beds and dressers from the thrift store. Everything appeared to be ready. That morning, Brent drove to the airport and I started making tuna fish sandwiches. An hour later, Brent opened the front door and in walked the most humble and sweet, small people I had ever seen. The parents and their six children were thin, exhausted and looked like life had almost been too much for them. Their oldest daughter was 14 and their youngest was 6. They didn't speak a word of English and we didn't speak a word of Laotian, but they understood they could trust me when I offered them tuna fish sandwiches and pineapple juice.

They had been so impoverished that we had to show them how to use the stove, refrigerator and indoor plumbing. The next day I took them to the grocery store so they could pick out foods they liked. They were overwhelmed at all the food in an American supermarket. They loved soy sauce and other spices and soon new smells from another world arose from the downstairs kitchen. Our seven year-old son, Rod, hit it off with their two younger boys ages 6 and 8. Rod loved their food and before long was eating dinner with them almost every day. He acquired the odor of soy sauce.

A few weeks after they arrived, the 14-year-old girl, Ahmpawong, came upstairs. Although her accent was thick, she picked up English quickly and we were communicating better. I noticed her legs were scarred and scaling. I pointed and asked her what had happened. In her own way, she explained to me she had been whipped in the refugee camp. I had some lotion nearby and asked if I could rub her legs to help with healing. She agreed and sat on the couch while I pulled up a chair.

As I gently treated Ahmpawong's legs she described the horrors of war . . . the massacres, the murders, how they had not slept through the night for six months due to gun shots and machine gun bursts. The family's escape was a miracle. Her father had been a Laotian military officer who refused to join the communists. He was ordered if he tried to escape the country, his family would suffer. But he knew that escaping was the only way his family would survive.

The Sutamawong family formulated a plan. They were constantly watched, so going anywhere with all eight of the children would arouse the suspicion that they were trying to escape. Therefore, they always left two children with grandparents when they went out. They sold their belongings and raised money to pay the boat runners who helped people escape across the Mekong River on dark moonless nights. It was dangerous business for all concerned. Each day the mother selected six of her eight children and walked with them to town. They bartered for food at the open market, but the real purpose was to receive notice when it was their night to escape. Finally notice came, tonight was the night. Mother hung around town until dark and then she slipped with six of her children into the jungle, infested with tigers, panthers and snakes. It was a moonless night offering escape under cover of darkness.

By midnight a considerable group had gathered at river's edge. The boat arrived and people were ordered to board silently. The greedy boat runners had scheduled too many people and the boat was jam-packed for the trip across the mile-wide river.

Halfway across, Mother heard Ahmpawong get knocked overboard. She could not see her daughter in the murky blackness and she dared not cry out lest the entire group be discovered and massacred. Fortunately, someone else was aware of a passenger forced overboard and, reaching out blindly, found an arm and pulled Ahmpawong back into the boat, saving her from certain capture, slavery, or death.

On the Thailand side of the river several nations had set up refugee camps. Ahmpawong and her family were taken into the French camp where they lived in tents for six months waiting for the father to escape and join them.

Bouhakam, the father, did escape—twice. Each time he swam the mile distance underwater, held down by rocks in a plastic bag tied to his belt and breathing through a long hollow reed. The first time he reached the Thai shore he was forced to swim back by French troops declaring their refugee camp was over quota. Sometime later he crossed the river again and, because he spoke some French, was allowed into the French refugee camp where he eventually found his wife and six children.

For six more months they remained in the camp waiting for a French citizen to sponsor them so they could start a new life in that country. Meanwhile they endured many sleepless nights due to communist machine gun raids into the camps, followed by beatings.

Finally the Laotian family was reassigned to an American sponsor in Chicago. On their way to America, that assignment was changed and they were sent to Utah. It had taken several years and several miracles for them to get here, but now we sat in safety as I held Ahmpawong's scarred foot in my hand. I felt so honored. I sensed that I was anointing the feet of a beautiful young angel with dark hair and brown skin. She had been through the unimaginable and by heaven's grace, we were given the opportunity to help her build a new life with her family in blessed America, "the land of the free!"

That day I asked Ahmpawong why we could hear her tiny 4'10" mother crying in the night. It was the cry only a mother can know for the two children she'd had to leave behind in Laos, two daughters, ages 16 and 4.

For six months in our home we nurtured and taught the Laotian family. Their English was improving, especially the kids who were doing well in school. Church members had helped by donating clothing and apartment furnishings. One member offered the parents jobs and rides to work. The Laotians had exceptionally fast hands. We were pleased with their progress and had become good friends.

Sponsors agree to help their refugees for at least two years and the goal is independence, financially and every other way. At the six month stage we asked our Laotian family if they felt ready to try living in America on their own, promising we would be nearby and continue to help them when needed. They were a little nervous, but excited to keep building their new life.

We found an inexpensive three-bedroom rental home, an old but reliable car and helped them get drivers' licenses. Our children and theirs were sad at the separation, but we arranged for them to get together frequently. These arrangements lasted to about the two-year mark. At some point things improved in Laos and mail service was restored. The family, Mom especially, was excited to receive a letter with a picture of the daughters, the older now 18 with her fiancé. Later pictures arrived of the wedding. The parents were saving money to bring their remaining children to America.

About this time the Laotians received additional news. Some Laotian relatives had escaped and were living in central California in an area where many Laotians had gathered. Before long our refugee family decided to join them. After many heartfelt hugs and thanks, our Laotian friends moved on to new adventures. We corresponded for several years, but then lost contact.

Baby Lost, Baby Returned

I have always sensed the moment of conception—the beginning of new life on earth—and was thrilled with my fifth pregnancy. Then, about the third month, I lost the baby to miscarriage. To have new life inside of me one moment and gone the next is a wrenching experience. I felt a very real presence had left me. I grieved over the loss of my child. I had felt this gentle female presence with me before she was even conceived.

During the three months her tiny body grew within me, her spirit self would occasionally enter my dreams and share with me her love. After the miscarriage, I feared that I had lost her forever. My yearning for her was constant.

Then God comforted me. I asked in prayer, "Will I have another child?" He whispered to my soul, "You will fulfill the measure of your creation."

About two months later I was shown in a dream that I had only lost this girl child temporarily . . . she would have another chance for birth through me. I saw her mature spirit. She was a woman dressed in white attire with brown hair pulled back at her neck and hanging down her back. Her large brown eyes were inquisitive. She appeared shy, even apprehensive about coming to earth, reluctant to leave behind the loving environment and special friends of her heavenly home.

However, in this dream she called me "Mother," and I knew that she was committing to come to me. I was greatly comforted and offered a prayer of gratitude to God for this understanding that she would still be born to me at a later time.

Several months later I had another dream. I saw myself in a hospital room. I was aware of every detail— the narrowness of the room, the window, the bed, the television. I saw the door open and a nurse walk in with a little bundle. I rejoiced when she placed a beautiful baby girl in my arms.

As I awakened from the dream, I sensed a divine, loving male presence standing in the doorway to my bedroom. In a distinct voice he declared of the female infant I had just seen in my dream, "Her name is Sarah. Her name is Sarah."

Not many days after this experience I conceived. During the critical third month of pregnancy, again I threatened to miscarry. The pain and hemorrhaging increased.

I fell to the floor and prayed with more intensity than I had ever prayed in my whole life. I was overwhelmed with flashbacks of the miscarriage I'd suffered the year before and the grief I'd endured. Why was this happening? I had been promised this time my daughter would come!

Eyes closed, prostrate on the floor, a scene unfolded in my mind. I saw my own spirit-self departing our heavenly home for earth. I was looking back as I moved swiftly away and saw our heavenly home bathed in what I can only describe as holy flames of bright white fire that did not consume. I knew that I had prepared for this journey for eons of time, but I was terrified. I didn't want to leave my Home. Separating from our Heavenly Father was heart-wrenching for me. I felt an intense sadness as I moved down through space. I was leaving a place where I had been safe and loved unconditionally for untold millennia, but I knew it was my time to embark on my mission to mortality.

As I continued traveling down through the stars, the pace accelerated. Then I saw it, the earth far, far below–foreboding, distant, cold—a stark contrast from heaven. I remembered being taught in my premortal life that earth was a long way from our heavenly home, but when I actually experienced the journey to earth, I was stunned by the cosmic distance.

I felt the chill of the approaching remote and dreary world. Fear and loneliness filled my being as the chasm widened from the nurturing, peaceful and loving environment of my premortal childhood. Comfort appeared in a presence, a strengthening escort who suddenly was by my side. Telepathically I conveyed to him, "I did not realize that the earth was so far away from our heavenly home."

"Indeed, it is a great distance," he acknowledged.

As the vision faded, a message of hope entered my mind: "You came to earth to be tested and tried, but you shall overcome the trial of this threatened miscarriage."

Reawakening to my immediate surroundings, I found myself in the most humble position of prayer I could imagine, flat on the floor. I sensed a Being of power enter the room. I felt compelled to rise. I cannot explain how, but I knew it was Jesus Christ. I was totally immersed in His love. I begged Him to heal my body for the sake of the child within me. In answer, He conveyed these words to my mind: "I am the Great Physician. I will heal your body and this baby will be born whole and well, for I have so decreed it."

The promise delivered, His presence gently withdrew. I laid down on the bed, enveloped in a peaceful, healing power. Soon, the pain and hemorrhaging stopped entirely. I was whole.

And, above all, my baby was safe! The following day, my doctor confirmed that everything was okay.

Months later when I went into labor, my husband drove me to the hospital. It was a cold, dark and rainy night. I closed my eyes to the soothing rhythm of the windshield wipers. In my mind I saw her—a beautiful woman with long brown hair and brown eyes. She was saying goodbye to many people, all dressed in white in the heavenly realm. I was eager to receive my promised namesake, little Sarah, but I could sense that she was again reluctant about leaving the unconditional love of her heavenly home. I feared there was a real chance she might withdraw from earth life again and I prayed for the safe arrival of our sweet daughter.

When I opened my eyes, we were just pulling into the hospital parking lot. I checked in and was wheeled to my room. The labor went normally. With my husband comforting me as best he could, I approached those final few minutes before giving birth when things get most challenging. I again closed my eyes and prayed silently. With my spiritual eyes, I saw the outline of a personage dressed in white, standing by my bed.

"I have personally escorted this child to mortality," he confirmed in my heart.

I was much relieved by this assurance that little Sarah would not "back out" again, that her apprehension for earth life was overcome by the aid of a divine escort. Shortly thereafter, our precious daughter was born.

Soon a nurse came in and reported, "Every room on the maternity floor is full. We have to move you down to an area on the second floor." I was taken on a gurney through long corridors and down elevators to an isolated little room. As they propped me up in my bed, mental images from a year earlier flooded my mind. I had seen this exact room in my dream, along with the events that followed.

The door opened and a nurse walked in with a little bundle and placed it in my arms. As I looked deeply into the eyes of my beautiful baby girl, it was as if I heard the proclaiming voice echo from the past, "Her name is Sarah. Her name is Sarah."

At last I held my namesake—Sarah Rebekah—the sweet baby of my dreams whose earthly body had miscarried on the first try, now returned to earth as promised.

Another Brother

When our daughter, Sarah Rebekah—or Becky, as we called her—was seven months old, she awakened from her naps with adorable cooing and singing. We joked among our family, (which included several foster daughters at the time), that Becky must be "talking with the angels." In my heart, I wondered if she really was.

One afternoon Becky announced with typical cooing that she had awakened from her nap. Approaching her room, I felt as if I was entering holy ground. I paused, and then quietly opened the door. Love filled the room and I sensed a gentle male presence hovering a few feet above Becky. I cannot say that I saw him with my natural eyes, but rather with some inner knowledge greater than sight. With my spiritual ears I heard him say, "Tell Mother I need to come now."

Becky babbled. She understood the message and was trying to communicate back to him. I knew instinctively this presence was our unborn son. He left the room only to return to me a month later in a dream to reemphasize it was time for his conception. Shortly afterward I conceived. Near the end of the third month during a meditative moment our son came again with the message, "My name is Matthew."

And I knew I would very soon be holding my son, a noble and loving spirit, one who would accomplish great things on this earth. This son we would name after Matthew Cowley.

Adoption

After the birth of Matthew Cowley David Hinze, we had six children and I felt our family was complete.

One day, I was pondering and praying for our Laotian family when the spirit came upon me and announced, "You will have another child. You are to name him Samuel. He is coming to you through adoption, but will come through your body."

I sat for a minute confused, "What does that mean?" Adoption?

But born through my body?

I shared my experience with Brent that night. "I think we're going to have another child through adoption." It was the only way I could make sense of it. Of course Brent, generous of heart and spirit, was willing to open our home again to another child.

Our Laotian family had opened my eyes to the fact that many in the world do not have the same rights and privileges as we in America. I had heard about China in the news and the conditions of living under a communist government. Studying China had become a passion for me.

For Christmas, Brent had given me a book on current Chinese politics and practices. Included were many large glossy photographs of the people and their living conditions. I became most concerned with the Chinese government's one-child policy. I didn't understand a government that could enforce such extreme laws, but after meeting the Laotian family I knew it was possible.

In China you could only have one child, unless you obtained an official birth permit, which was rare. Forced abortions were rampant in the practice of infanticide, a procedure where women are forced by the government to abort their children. Chinese abortion vans drive through neighborhoods, arresting noncompliant pregnant mothers and transporting them to forced abortion clinics.

I researched Chinese orphanages. It saddened me greatly that if a Chinese woman became pregnant with a second child without a birth permit, she might be able to hide and give birth to the child, but she could not keep it. Out of fear she had to take the child to an orphanage after birth, or even do the unthinkable and abandon them in a garbage bin so she and her family would not be punished through taxes, prison or other penalties. I wanted to rescue a Chinese baby.

The Other Side of the Country

Brent accepted a job in Washington D. C. and with our children, we moved from our small Utah town to a suburb in Virginia. Within weeks, I started making phone calls, inquiring how I could adopt a baby from China. Brent asked daily when he returned from work. "Any progress on the adoption?"

But things weren't moving as fast as I hoped. Then, one evening after putting the kids to bed, Brent and I prayed. We felt urgency about finding this child to adopt.

For a second time the impression came to me, "You will have another child. You are to name him Samuel. He is coming to you through adoption, but will come through your body."

Suddenly, I understood and explained to Brent, "I believe there is a child who wants to come to earth and for some reason the assigned mother cannot have him."

But maybe heaven can reassign babies. Although not originally intended for us, it was clear to me that heaven's plans had changed for this soul. In America, we have the precious freedoms to choose the number of children we want."

At that moment, I felt the eyes of another child on me. Then Brent felt it. Although Brent was always ready to receive and provide for any children Heavenly Father wanted to send us, he was protective of my health and my burdens and left the timing of each pregnancy up to me. That day for the first time in our marriage he took the initiative and said, "I think we should have another baby." Our beautiful baby boy, Samuel Lawrence, was born nine months later in Fairfax, Virginia.

The question—"Do some children become reassigned to a sort of Plan B because their Plan A didn't work out?"—would be dealt with later when many cases of this nature came to my attention in my work with prebirth studies.

Curiously, as we welcomed Samuel into our family, I felt he had been reassigned to us, not from China, but from Argentina.

Virginia was much different from Utah, but within the walls of our home it was as it had always been. One Christmas Tadd and Rod received huge boxes of Legos from Santa, but that wasn't the only present planned for them. For the two weeks of Christmas break, we gave them the living room. They could build their Lego cities, houses, farms, and towns without having to put them away at the end of each day.

One Sunday afternoon our bishop from church came to visit. We informed him that he would need to enter Legoland to find a seat. He did and thought it was cool. My children were my best friends. Now there was nothing I enjoyed more then to be a stay- at-home mom.

Rod's Injury and Healing

I was making the kids' favorite dinner, pigs in a blanket (hot dogs wrapped in crescent rolls) when Tadd ran in the front door and said, "Mommy, Rod's lying in the street and he won't get up."

"Tell him to get out of the street," I said. "He won't."

By now I sensed something serious was going on. A memory flashed through my mind. A few months earlier in winter I'd been impressed my sons were in danger. There were woods and streams and frozen ponds everywhere. In spite of Rod and Tadd being instructed to ask before they went anywhere, they had this frustrating habit of taking off on their bikes without telling me.

I had driven around that day in the family van and finally spotted their bikes in the bushes. I parked and walked through the trees. Suddenly there they were, the little clowns, literally playing on thin ice out in the middle of a wintry pond. I hollered at them to come off the ice and never do that again. Now, it sounded like my son was again in danger.

My baby Sam was two weeks old and asleep in his bassinet, but I grabbed the keys and ran out to the car. Tadd jumped in beside me and told me what had happened.

"Rod and his friend dared each other to jump on the back of a UPS truck," he said. "It stopped at the stop sign. His friend jumped off before it started moving again, but Rod held on until the truck was going fast and he fell off."

Tadd pointed the way down the street when I noticed cars had stopped and several people were standing over a body.

I was numb. There laid my son, non-responsive and bleeding from the ears. I went up to the paramedic and said, "I'm his mother."

Rod was carefully moved onto a stretcher. Because of rush hour traffic in Washington D.C., he was taken to the hospital in a helicopter. Before he was whisked away, I knelt near him and whispered, "God, please don't let him die, please don't let him die."

A lady from my neighborhood offered to take me to the hospital. On the car ride over, I was praying with all my heart that my son would live. I felt some reassurance when I heard in my mind, "He won't die. He has not yet fulfilled his mission upon the earth."

I arrived in the hospital waiting room and heard my son screaming in the other room. Although he was distraught, it was comforting to hear his voice. Brent was contacted at work and arrived at the hospital as quickly as he could. We entered the intensive care room and looked at our son, all hooked up to monitors. He had two black eyes, his body bruised and he'd suffered head trauma. They weren't sure how long he would be in a coma.

"When he awakes, he's going to have some lingering effects from the fall," the doctor said. "We just don't know how bad it will be."

I kept a constant daily vigil by his bedside, while Brent took the night shift. Friends took care of our children at home. Every day was harder than the last. I kept up the hope, but I'd heard stories of people staying in comas for months before finally awakening with severe brain damage.

By the seventh day, I was desperate. Rod was pale and looked like a sick little boy, nothing like the athletic 4th grader I had known a week ago. His hair was tousled, but the twinkle in his eyes and his sweet grin was gone. When I was in the room alone with him, I took his hand and prayed with all the intensity of my heart.

"Let me take his injury," I pleaded with the Lord. "I need him back, whole and perfect. Please hear my request."

Within minutes, Rod opened his eyes. "I'm hungry, Mom," he said. "Can I have a hamburger and french fries?"

My Rodney was back and the doctor's couldn't find a thing wrong with him. Rod thought his black bruised eyes made him look cool, but he didn't remember anything about the incident of falling. After 10 days in the hospital, we took Rod home. The doctors let us know he might have some post-traumatic stress show up later, including panic attacks and anxiety. However, the Lord took me at his word. I was the one who developed these symptoms, not Rod.

Soon I had my first of many panic attacks that lasted off and on for months. My heart raced and I felt like I was going to die. I broke out in cold sweats. I started having anxiety day and night. Only prayer got me through each incident. The doctors seemed to be at a loss to know how to help me.

I later told Brent about my prayer in the hospital, how I had prayed to carry Rod's burden for him.

"Sarah, don't ever pray that kind of prayer again," he said. "The Lord took that prayer literally at your word. You now have every symptom the doctors said Rod would have. Next time, just pray the Lord will heal him and don't take it on you."

I agreed that was wise counsel, but in the heat of a crisis, a mother will sometimes do anything for her child.

Writing for *Welcome Home*

With Samuel finally sleeping through the night, the nursing demands diminished. I was more rested, and I had a bit more clarity of mind. I learned of a group of women who enjoyed writing, even if they were amateurs. I joined them and then had to figure out what it was I needed to write.

Searching for a writing topic was kind of like a game Brent and I played with our children called Bulla Bulla. We took turns where one of us would leave the room while the others hid something like a small toy, a pen, etc. When the person was called back into the room to hunt for the hidden object, the rest of us would begin chanting "Bulla Bulla."

If the person moved away from the object the Bulla Bullas got softer and slower. When the seeker moved toward the hidden object, the Bulla Bullas got louder and faster until when they practically on top of the object we were virtually shouting BULLA BULLA as loud and fast as possible. When the object was found, we all clapped and cheered. Then it was somebody else's turn.

Well, as I said, finding what the Lord wanted me to write was a bit like Bulla Bulla. In the beginning I felt far away and could hardly hear or feel the approval of the Spirit. As my search led me closer to the right topic, the whisperings got stronger. The Lord knew I would continue to seek His guidance until I succeeded.

My growing group of young mother writers learned of my interests and concerns. They recommended that I make contact with Cherie Loveless, one of the founders and publishers of a delightful publication called *Welcome Home,* a monthly newsletter that went into the homes of thousands of young mothers across the country. I called and spoke with Cherie and she invited me to meet for lunch. Before our meeting concluded, Cherie invited me to be a part of her editorial staff. Suddenly I had a position as a writer, small though it was.

I assigned myself writing days on which I obtained a babysitter for my now seven children and locked myself in my bedroom to write for a few hours. Three years had passed since my last publication and I was excited to have the opportunity again. In my first article I wrote it as if I was standing at a window looking in on my life as a young mother, and the article was well-received.

The Day We Cleaned the Closet

For some reason I dreaded cleaning out my son Matthew's closet. It was a huge task, one that I had put off for weeks. I knew I would find various assortments of animate and inanimate objects, judging from the slight odor coming from the room (probably leftovers from last week's play tea party that had been sneaked upstairs.)

It usually took me almost three hours each morning to get Brent and our other five children (two in junior high and three more in elementary school), out the door. This left Matthew, age three years, and Samuel, age eight months, as my morning companions.

By 10 a.m. Samuel was usually ready to snuggle back down in his bed for a nap, leaving Matthew and me with some time together, so I squared my shoulders and got on with the task.

One reason Matthew's closet had gotten so messy was that Matthew loved to play dress-up. With two older brothers, Tadd and Rod, he had acquired quite a lot of hand-me-downs—old Star Wars shirts, plenty of clip-on ties, (the kind designed to cause pain) and an assortment of belts and boots. He put together an amazing display of clothes, came downstairs to the kitchen, and with a big grin said, "Hi Mom! How do I look?"

"Wow, Matty! You look great! Who are you dressed up like today?"

"Daddy."

Then he would describe to me why he picked a certain vest to match his blue rain boots. And such was how we pass many mornings.

After the dress-up clothes come off each day, Matthew usually dumped them in a pile in the closet. The pile had grown quite large. We sorted through the clothes together, and Matty helped me fold the clean ones and put them in his drawer. The dirty ones went into the laundry pile.

Soon we worked our way down to the book boxes. As the sixth child, Matty had acquired an amazing collection of Little Golden Books, along with others. Since one never throws out books or buttons without thoughtful pondering, we first began sorting through the treasures. In one corner we discovered a huge pile of old coloring books, some going back eight or ten years to our oldest girls, Krista and Laura. As I came across an unusually pretty colored cow or flower, I pointed it out to Matty, and he would do the same with me. Soon we sorted out what was worth saving and then we began to organize the books into various categories. Before long the book boxes were beautiful.

I chuckled as I wondered just how many hours this would stay in order. Somehow it didn't matter that it would not last; the important thing was for "one brief shining moment" I could reflect back on the day the books were organized. I recalled my mother- in-law telling me about a friend of hers who kept her linen closet so organized that she tied every bundle with pink satin ribbons. I may not get to the linen closet for a few more years, but I would challenge any mother of a three-year-old to have a neater closet than Matty's. Why, it was beautiful!

Then we found the Mickey Mouse Sticker Book. I must have bought it three children back, because it was old, but as soon as Matty spotted it, he wanted it. I helped him carefully tear out the stickers and then find the right page for him to stick each in its place. We licked, sticked, and admired our beautiful creation. Then with one sudden burst of energy, Matty jumped up, threw his chubby little arms around my neck, gave me a big kiss and said, "Mommy, I love you. I really do."

As I looked deeply into those beautiful brown eyes, my own filled with tears. I felt joy and a deep sense of oneness with my three-year-old treasure.

"Oh, Matty, I love you too," I said. "I'm so glad that you are my little boy."

With that we smiled, giggled a little, and went back to our discussion of the sticker book.

As simple as it may seem, we formed another bond of closeness and commitment that day. Now that Matthew is grown, I still remember that day. I'm grateful I was there with my son to enjoy that fleeting moment, and to capture it in my heart to savor with other treasured times with my family. In my mind, my brown-eyed child will dance across my memory and delight me forever with his three-year-old wonder.

Finding a Home in Arizona

We had lived for two years near the nation's capitol when Brent accepted a job in Arizona. Once again, we packed up the moving truck and drove across the country to our new desert home. We rented a small home we intended to buy, but at the last minute the sale didn't go through.

The original homeowners decided not to sell their home and informed us we had two weeks to move out. The stress was too much and one afternoon, while my children were playing next door with the neighbors, I rested on the couch and fell asleep. I dreamed of a home. There was a large yard surrounded with tall pine trees with plenty of room for our children to play. I awoke in a startle with this impression: "If you will get in your car and drive, you will be led to your new home."

Knowing my children were in good care, I jumped in the car and started driving through the neighborhood. At each corner, I would stop and listen. "Do I turn left or right?" I would say in my mind. Each time an impression told me which way to turn. In a matter of minutes, I was in a neighborhood I had frequently driven through. I felt it was the most beautiful street in our town, but certainly not an area Brent and I could afford.

Suddenly I saw a "For Sale" sign in a yard. The property was overgrown with tall grass and unkempt bushes, obviously vacant. I parked my car in the driveway and walked up to the windows of the home, pushing the bushes aside so I could peek inside. I walked around to the other side of the house where I saw a large side yard, surrounded with pine trees, the yard from my dreams. That sweet sound of wind whistling through the trees caught my attention as a voice entered my mind: "The Lord is going to give you this home."

We contacted the realtor who reported that the owner had moved out of state where he had purchased another home. He was running out of money making two house payments, so he had just dropped the price on the Arizona home by $40,000, hoping it would sell quickly.

We could hardly believe our ears. This home would normally have been out of our price range, but now, with the Lord's help, we might qualify. We took the whole family to see the home that evening. When the realtor opened the door we were hit with a musty odor, but our kids rushed from room to room, getting more excited as they went along. When they saw the pool and the half- acre side-yard "football field," they were sold. We had to make an offer to avoid family mutiny!

The miracle happened and within a few days or so, we moved in on a lease option, and in a few months, we were blessed to purchase the home. The Hinze Hacienda has been our family home now for more than 25 years.

Our growing family in 1974. Krista and Laura, and pregnant with baby Rod.

*Family photo taken in 1987 when we first moved to Arizona. Pictured
are Rod, Krista, Laura, Becky, Sarah (with Samuel on my lap), Brent,
Matthew, Tadd.*

*Elva Cowley, in her new petite dress suit,
holding our son Matthew Cowley Hinze.*

My 38th birthday photo--taken as a present for my mom and dad. I had a tradition to send my mom a present on my birthday each year to thank her for giving me life.

June 1990. The two daughters I had felt near me years earlier were now in my arms—new baby Anna Adele with big sister Rachel Elizabeth.

At a family reunion in Beaver, Utah after the long ride in The Eldorado Van. Laura, Krista, Brent, Becky, Samuel, Sarah (holding Rachel), Tadd, Matthew, and Rod.

Mom and Dad take a break from working in the garden, one of their favorite pastimes.

PART III

HOW HAVE MEMORIES OF ANGELS SAVED LIVES?

My Writing Tradition

I remember gray skies in Tennessee, when the rain rolled over the mountains and into my backyard. Thunder would start to grumble sometime in the early evening and soon the rain drops would start their pattering. On warm evenings, Mom would open the front door and I could hear the rain run down the walkway. Most nights, dinner included fresh garden picks from dad's garden; sliced tomatoes (Mom always salted them), cucumbers and green beans, pork chops or fried chicken with gravy, some potato pancakes fried up in oil and washed down with fresh milk. The menu varied but it was always delicious home cooking prepared with care from mom—one of the ways she loved us best. Then many evenings we would go out on the porch and watch the rain.

Rain was nature's way of keeping me in the moment. Everything seemed to come alive. I would watch the morning glories that were climbing the front porch trellis fill up and droop with the weight of rain water. Little streams seemed to form and drip down the thin vines. Squirrels would run from tree to tree and birds chirped across the roadways. I felt safe and lonely at the same time.

I remember those times on the porch like I was there yesterday. Dad would read the newspaper while mom caught up on her sewing all the while rocking in the porch swing together. Sometimes we would talk about the events of the day. My little sister Sandy usually had a book in her lap.

It was a simple time.

As a mother, I tried to create simplicity for my children, moments where they could be in the now and feel the strength of the world around them, but there were no front porches in Arizona and very few rainy days. Dinner was inside with the air- conditioning turned to a cool 78 degrees. Not many days with the screen door open either. I was a long way from home. It wasn't that I missed Tennessee, I loved my life in the desert, but I realized how special and magical the days of childhood were.

And I realized that it was the tradition of being together on the porch those rainy evenings that made the experience so special. It was watching my parents, hearing their quiet conversations and knowing I had a family that loved me.

I kept up the tradition of home cooking because for me, it was like a communion of love from my hands to my husband and our children's tummies. Dinner time was noisy and busy but we always wanted to hear about our children's goals and experiences. We encouraged them to reach out to their friends and new kids, especially those whom they thought might be lonely. I learned to make tie comforters for my kid's beds (although most nights a sheet was enough to keep them warm). Reading, hugging and tucking them into bed night after night became a familiar pattern.

Traditions seemed to find their way into my home and eventually, into my writing.

A 4 a.m. writing schedule was born. I set my internal alarm clock and many mornings, I would open my eyes at 4 a.m. on the button. This was the only time the house was quiet and I had a few uninterrupted hours where I could write.

Later, with the children in school, I arranged my day to have time to write. Sudden strokes of ideas could come at anytime— while driving around a van full of kids to gymnastics or soccer, while watching television or reading a book to my children. I had to learn to simplify my life to have time to receive inspiration if and when it came, therefore a note pad and pencil were never too far away. I learned that inspiration is like the wind—it can come and go so briefly that if not captured swiftly, it may never return.

Meeting Joan

The summer of 1990 will be remembered for the broken air-conditioner and frizzy hair. Finances were tight, so instead of putting out the thousands of dollars for a new unit, Brent decided to open the trap doors in the ceiling that housed the old swamp cooler (swamp being the operative word). It hadn't been used for years. Have you ever been sucked into a wind tunnel? Then spit out? Have you ever walked around in wet sticky clothes all day? That's a swamp cooler.

A swamp cooler forced me to ponder how the early settlers of Arizona ever survived without air-conditioning. A swamp cooler doesn't just hum, it roars, so those sweet nights of dinner conversation turned into "What did you say?" and "I can't hear you!" On the bright side, it cut down on yelling across the house.

Laura had just graduated from high school and was working as a preschool teacher in a local daycare center when she met Joan. Joan was from the East Coast, animated and friendly. After they had a few conversations at school, Laura felt impressed to introduce me to Joan. We became instant friends and soon I handed her my manuscript, *Life before Life*. Later she called, "I can't believe this, but now that I've read your book I realized I had a prebirth experience too."

She shared with me the following story:

Clearing away the morning dishes on a beautiful warm and sunny spring day, I was feeling an amazing contentment with my life. My husband and I had a new home, a beautiful family and a wonderful marriage. It seemed that we had everything anyone could want or need. When the doorbell rang and interrupted my thought, I assumed that it was my neighbor. She had phoned earlier in the day about a lost dog and mentioned that she would soon be over. When I opened the door, there stood a strange man. Before I realized what I had done, I had allowed him into my home. He said he needed to use my phone because of car troubles. I knew immediately that I had placed myself in great danger. Before I had time to think, he was pointing a gun at me. I was in a daze as he proceeded to assault me. After locking me in my bathroom, the stranger ransacked my house. A feeling of great calm overcame me.

I asked the Lord, "Please, if this man is going to kill me, let it be swift. Please take care of my family and please carry their grief."

My fear began to totally vanish and I felt a presence by me. Although I saw no one, the presence was unmistakably that of a gentle and kind young woman. I said out loud, "Who are you?"

I sensed that this spirit essence was a blood relative and I assumed that this was a guardian angel that was going to take me to the other side should I be killed. The presence was so powerful, that I knew this person was in charge of the situation now, not the criminal. My mind was not on the criminal, although he was still in my home. My mind was on this unseen person who was with me.

Finally, I heard the intruder leave and almost immediately thereafter, I felt my spiritual friend depart.

I managed to unlock the bathroom door and then ran outside my house. As the sun warmed my face, I felt so thankful to be alive! I thought, "Thank you God, for letting me live. I will be O.K."

I never spoke to anyone about my experience with the unseen comforter—partly because it was very personal in nature. The focus now was on the crime and the opportunity did not arise to talk about the female spirit.

Ten months later, after six and a half years of wanting another child, I was delighted to find myself pregnant. I knew I was having a girl. I told my doctor, my friends and relatives. There was no doubt in my mind, although many of them teased me for my confidence. On the night my baby was born, as I was experiencing this great miracle take place, it was almost like there was an aura around the baby's head. All attending were in awe at the beauty of this great occasion.

When the doctor had cleaned her off somewhat and made sure she was breathing well, he placed her in my arms. It was as though everyone else in the room faded in the background and she and I were alone. I looked into her eyes and her focus caught mine. Her little eyes became transfixed on me and we had an immediate bond.

I whispered "It was you."

No one else knew what I meant, but I knew she did.

It was very strange to have this precious little life—so new—and yet for me to have the knowledge of the strength and power of her spirit. It was as though she had been watching me for a long time. I felt this child had been my protector since before birth.

The Lord bore witness to me that this day was the reason my life was spared so that I could bring her to earth. No matter what other honors may come to me throughout my life, my greatest accomplish will be that of being granted the opportunity of being a mother.

What a miracle it was to watch as the Lord sent people like Joan into my life. With her permission, I used her story in *Life before Life*.

One day, Joan called Laura at work with a secret suggestion. "Let's nominate your mom for an award. I'll take care of everything, if you just give me a bit of information," she said.

Laura was more then happy to help with the application. It was certainly a surprise when I received a call from a group called the National Eagle Forum in Illinois. I had been chosen to receive the Arizona Homemaker of the Year Award. I was told, "If possible, we would like you and your husband to come to Washington, D.C. and receive the award in person."

When I told the kids, they laughed. "You? You're just an ordinary mom who's still in your robe at noon."

I couldn't argue with that logic, but felt maybe the Lord had granted me this opportunity to move the book forward and put me in a position to meet people and make contacts to help the unborn.

I had spent so many years pregnant and nursing, that I had nothing nice to wear. Day to day, a wardrobe of stretch-waist pants and stained shirts was something a Homemaker of the Year would wear, but I wanted to look my best. The roar of the swamp cooler reminded me I had no money to spend on anything new, when a friend of mine called. "I have a beautiful suit you should borrow," she said. She invited me into her home and I went on a shopping spree in her closet.

Brent and I made arrangements and were soon on our way to the East Coast. I took my manuscript with me and hoped to collect more information and stories.

The evening of the awards, I left our hotel room early to go downstairs to save us seats. Brent arrived late and told me that there was a big commotion in the lobby of the hotel. Presidential candidate Bill Clinton was there with his entourage checking into the hotel. Their security team had held up those wanting to get inside.

The presidential campaign of 1992 was in full swing and the battle of pro-life and pro-choice was a big part of it. I knew the unborn would be in greater jeopardy if Clinton won the presidency and found it ironic that he was staying in the same hotel as me. He had his agenda and I had mine.

The dinner and the awards ceremony went off without a hitch. When Phyllis Schalfly, the director of National Eagle Forum, shook my hand and handed me the award, I could feel her powerful spirit, and the impression came to my mind, "There stands a modern-day Esther."

Esther's story is one of my favorite stories in the Bible. She made a courageous stand to defend her people, the Jews, during a time of great political turmoil and civil uprising. Her defense of them literally saved their lives. The Lord told Esther that she came to the earth "for such a time as this." (Esther 4:14)

After the dinner and festivities, we were exhausted and headed to our room. I plopped down on the bed, evening clothes and all, and closed my eyes just to rest for a bit while Brent took some time to read and relax in the other room. At that moment, it was as if my spirit traveled and I was taken away. In a place of great heavenly beauty, I heard the following words:

The Lord is grateful for your attention to write and to be a voice for unborn children. This mission is under His guiding care and will be unfolded according to His will. Many spirit children of God are concerned with the treacherous journey to come to the earth and receive a body. You are called to help them. You will be guided line upon line what to do. If you do this, you and your family will be blessed beyond measure.

I don't know how long I was gone, but in an instant, I was back. Brent was still in the other room reading. I opened my eyes and tried to understand what had happened to me. This was not a dream—this was more.

Something changed that night. A realization of what I needed to do had been imprinted on my mind. I knew without a doubt, that this impossible mission would be guided and directed by the Savior himself.

Becoming a Memory Catcher

I had learned by personal experience that our unborn children can serve as guardian angels and they can make contact with their future parents or others. These contacts may occur in dreams in which the unborn soul announces it is their time to be born. For years researchers in the social sciences referred to contacts with the unborn as "announcing dreams."

Announcing dreams have been identified in cross-cultural studies all over the world. Because I had learned that contacts with the unborn can occur in more ways than just dreams, and because the contacts can include more than just the announcement of the impending birth or conception, I began calling these spiritual contacts "prebirth experiences" or PBE's.

Science may be viewed as man's efforts to discover, systematize and make use of things already known by God. The eminent scientist, Sir Isaac Newton, once said that he was like a child studying a few pebbles on the shore, while the great limitless sea was before him. As a researcher in a new field, I related to Newton's sense of awe. The prebirth studies are so profound that we would be shortchanging ourselves—and the unborn—if we fail to analyze them for the truths that they hold.

A prebirth experience may be thought of as the opposite end of the spectrum from the near death experience. The near death experience give insights as to where we go when we leave the earth through death, whereas the prebirth experience gives insight on where we come from before birth.

During this time, my love of the ancient texts, the Dead Sea Scrolls and the Nag Hammadi Texts, became another passion. I was intrigued to learn that these ancient cultures knew and wrote about our pre-earth life with God. They understood that we came to the earth, not by chance, but under a divine plan and that we were created as spirit beings, literal children of God, before our birth and conception. One of my favorite texts from The Book of Thomas is a quote attributed to Jesus: "If they say to you, from where have you originated? Say to them, we have *come from the light*, where the Light has originated through itself. If they say to you, who are you? Say, we are His sons [and daughters] and we are the elect of the Living Father."

I was convinced my next assignment in my writing mission was to bring to the world's attention the marvelous phenomenon of the "prebirth experience." But how would I find enough individuals who'd had prebirth experiences to do a real study of this phenomenon?

Today I receive most new cases online through my website www. sarahhinze.com and through my e-mail sarahhinze.hinze@gmail.com, but I began my quest before internet was available. So I did it the old-fashioned way—I wrote letters to newspaper editors across America and a few foreign countries and they published my requests. At first I heard nothing and was a bit disappointed. I prayed harder for God's help in my research and finally came the first phone call, then the first letter.

The accounts were amazing and poignant. In some cases, the contributors wrote up their experience and mailed it to me. For others I took notes, wrote up their account and mailed or read it to them over the phone for their approval. Soon Brent was on board. His talent and background as a social scientist helped tremendously. Some wanted their name attached to their story, others preferred anonymity.

I discovered a curious correlation in my research. A number of prebirth experiences occurred during near death experiences. In these cases the individual would die, their spirit would cross over into the Light, and one of the things they were shown was their unborn future children. Often they remembered knowing their future children before they came to the earth, how they had been great friends and loved one another for eons of time, and how they had promised, when assigned to come to earth first, they would become the parents of these beloved souls when it was their time for birth.

To build my network of resources, during each interview I always asked, "Do you know anyone else who has had a prebirth experience that I might contact?" Within months I had about 150 case studies of prebirth experiences, roughly the same number of near death experiences Dr. Raymond Moody had when he published the now classic bestseller about where we go at death, *Life after Life*. I decided to title my first book about where we come from, *Life before Life*.

Finding a Publisher

Breaking into the publishing world is a challenging experience. Entire books have been written about the process so I will not belabor the point here. Fortunately, my material was intriguing enough that several publishers expressed an interest. I signed with a small publishing house. I was naïve, to say the least, but excited. I hoped my book would be read and shared all around the world. Imagine my feelings of awe when I saw my first book, *Life before Life,* on display in 1993 at a bookseller's convention in Salt Lake City. Conference attendees were eager to read it and what a thrill to finally hold it in my hands. It was almost as good as holding a newborn. I envisioned big things from that book.

However, marketing and distribution of the book was limited. It received some nice reviews in a few newspapers, sold about 5,000 copies, and then gradually sunk into the sea of new books published annually. Although *Life before Life* did not become a best seller, it did get my name out their as a researcher. I received phone calls, letters and visits from people who gained a new sense of purpose in life for themselves and their families. Some even said the book saved lives when plans for abortion or suicide were no longer considered when the reader gained a better understanding of our purpose here on earth.

So as the memories rolled in faster than ever, I went right to work on another book I titled *Coming from the Light*. In May, 1995, my publisher and I took it to the American Booksellers Convention in Chicago. My friend, Richard Paul Evans, (author of the bestseller *The Christmas Box)* was in the next booth. I said to him "Richard, I need to get my book into the hands of a New York publisher for bigger distribution. What should I do?"

He looked me square in the eyes and said, "You go out on that floor with your book in hand and you find yourself a young, enthusiastic female agent."

I thanked him for his counsel, grabbed some business cards, and started walking blindly. I was in a room the size of two football fields with tables and booths and people rushing around in every which direction. Talk about looking for a needle in a haystack! After staring at scores of people, and talking to several more, suddenly I stopped a woman, literally in her tracks. I read her name badge and saw she was a literary agent. I gave her my three-minute elevator pitch. She was interested and asked for a copy of my book, which I handed her.

"Here's my card," she said. "We'll be in touch."

The book went from one agent to another until finally it was sold to Simon & Schuster's Pocket Books division. They bought the paperback rights to *Coming from the Light* with release date of January 1997. I couldn't believe it.

I soon had an editor at Pocket Books call me and say, "Your book is coming out in a few days. Are you ready for a best seller? No one knows what makes a best seller, but there's one quality we always look for. When you pick up the book, you can't put it down because it is just that good. Sarah, your book has that quality."

I finally felt I had a book that would go around the world. Then a call came from *People* magazine. I braced myself, knowing this could be my big break. I was told *People* was considering my book for a cover story, but they were also considering a story about a man who had seen his childhood dog in heaven during a near-death experience.

I waited several very long days for another call, but I never did hear back from *People*. Imagine my glare in the grocery store a few months later when I saw *People* featuring a man holding a photograph of his dead dog. It was disappointing to come so close and then to lose out on powerful publicity.

Going to New York

Having a book published by Simon & Schuster was not a small deal. I was invited to speak at the Learning Annex in New York City with four

New York Times best-selling authors. I was a replacement for Dr. Melvin Morse, who couldn't attend. I was to give a 90- minute lecture, and that daunting task left me a bit numb.

I asked Brent to go with me, hoping he would finish my talk if I died at the podium, because I was actually envisioning myself being carried off in a stretcher. I prepared a 22-page talk with my best stories, then I practiced and rehearsed until I had it nearly memorized. Brent agreed to go, and we flew to New York.

Like football players going into the stadium to check everything out before the Super Bowl, I walked to the Learning Annex ballroom across the street from Times Square. The room was prepared for the following day of events. At least 400 chairs were up in the ballroom with a gorgeous chandelier hanging overhead. I couldn't believe I was in New York City.

I thought of my children at home and wondered, "How did I ever get here? Was my small voice going to be sophisticated enough for this tough New York crowd? Would they like my message? Would it be accepted?"

The next day, authors Paul Perry and Dannion Brinkley spoke first and received a warm reception as well as standing ovations. The pressure was on. Now it was my turn. I walked up on the stage, numb but enthusiastic. The room was full of professionals dressed in three-piece suits and designer clothes. Were these sophisticated people here to listen to a mother talk about unborn babies? I had prayed much for God's support. In front of this crowd I feared I would stumble saying my name, but I was blessed with the gift I had prayed for—I felt poised and articulate.

I opened with a humorous story regarding Dr. Kenneth Ring who sat in the audience as the next speaker. He was a pioneer researcher and author on the near-death studies. I had sent him a copy of my manuscript months earlier, hoping he'd endorse my work. I called him at his University of Connecticut office one morning and left a message. Later, my phone rang, but I assumed the call was for one of my teenage daughters. Rachel, my five-year old came to me a few minutes later. "Mommy, there's a man on the phone who wants to talk to you, but I'm having fun playing office with him."

I ran to the phone and picked up the receiver. "Sarah, this is Dr. Ring calling from the University of Connecticut. I've had a lot of fun talking with your daughter. She'll be a great receptionist someday. How many children do you have?"

"Dr. Ring, I have nine children," I stammered.

"Nine! I know that you love children, but nine?" he said with levity in his voice. "Oh, did Rachel tell you? I'd be happy to endorse your book."

I shared this story with ease and Dr. Ring smiled warmly. I had great respect for Dr. Ring. He related to my collection of prebirth experiences because he reported in his books that some people have physical and emotional healing after reading stories of spiritually transforming experiences. In other words, you don't have to nearly die to be transformed. You can read an account of someone who has experienced a powerful experience and become equally transformed.

After my lecture, I received a standing ovation. I walked into the audience and shook many hands. The audience loved the material and many were obviously emotionally moved. I visited the rest of the day with conference attendees, gathering more ideas and experiences.

One lady said, "I never knew I was a child of God. Thank you for teaching me that." Another beautiful young woman said, "While you were talking, I understood something I never knew before. I've had five abortions. That was wrong, wasn't it? What can I do about it?"

I was shocked that someone could have an abortion and not understand the real impact of it. We had about 30 seconds to talk. "There is hope," I said. "Jesus wants to forgive you, but you have to work it out with Him in prayer. I know you can do it."

I autographed and sold every one of the 200 copies of *Coming from the Light* that my publisher had sent to the event. My hand ached and my face was frozen in a permanent smile. Finally, my book was out there and well-received. I felt I had launched.

Angel Mania

About that time, *Touched by an Angel* was the #1 television show in America. Many networks featured shows on miracles and heaven. Mainstream media was becoming more comfortable talking about heaven. Over the next few years my research was featured on ten television shows.

In one instance, a producer named Joe from the television show *Extra* called. He wanted to feature my research on his show.

Extra was a bit like the television show *Entertainment Tonight*, with many Hollywood features. Before I would have jumped at the opportunity to be on television and share this book with anyone who would listen, but now I hesitated. These stories were so reverent—even sacred—and I didn't want them featured between segments of actresses dress styles and diet tips for bikini season. Would they sensationalize my work or take liberties with it that I never intended? I didn't want to do it and expressed my concerns to Joe. He listened and seemed to get a better understanding of the criteria I needed.

"We will do the feature how you want it done," he assured me, and in two weeks the camera crew was knocking on my front door. Joe called and told me the feature was scheduled to air on Good Friday. He later reported, "Of all the segments I have ever worked on, this is the one I am most proud of."

It was a proud day for me too. The show was very tastefully done and I was pleased. As far as I know, I was the only mother in the neighborhood who in the morning had done her grocery shopping with five children bouncing off the grocery cart and in the evening was featured on primetime television.

Calmed by a Dove

Another television producer from the show *Angels and Miracles* called and asked if he could send a crew to interview me for his show. The director hired a local camera crew and was scheduled to arrive at 10 a.m. on a Sunday morning. I was up early and getting ready when I walked into the foyer by the front door. I stopped short. There was a baby dove on the entry table sitting calmly beneath a large painting of Christ.

How? I looked around. *The front door wasn't even open. Morning doves, friendly, cooing little gray and white birds, are daily visitors to our front lawn. But how did this little bird get inside?*

I carefully picked up the baby bird and stood quietly, bewildered. The bird was totally calm . . . holding it seemed to bring peace to my anxious heart. He looked up at me with his tiny little eyes as if he were offering me a blessing. Through this tiny creature, I felt the blessings of God would be with me as I worked on the day's filming. I was nervous and didn't like being the focus. Although I was grateful to share my message, working on television features wasn't my favorite thing to do. I always had a bit of anxiety before I filmed.

I looked at the baby bird and allowed his calm energy to fill my heart. I finally walked out my front door and put the bird on the branch of a nearby tree. It hopped on and I whispered, "Can you go find your mommy?" The little bird took off like a shot to the very top of the grandfather pine tree in our yard.

At 10 a.m. the doorbell rang and I invited the director, the camera crew, and their miles and miles of electrical cords into my house. Everything that goes with sound, lighting and filming was now set up in my living room and I was invited to sit on a chair in the middle of it. "Please introduce yourself," the director said. "State your full name and then spell it."

I was familiar with this routine. "My name is Sarah Hinze," I began when *pop*, *pop*, *pop*—every light in the room shut off.

"What's going on?" the director asked.

"The sound is down too," the guy behind the camera said. "And my camera isn't working either."

They looked into the next room where the lights were still on. I knew what was going on. I said, "I think I have an idea what has happened. There's energy with this work that sometimes affects electrical equipment."

I said no more, but could feel the force of spirit children entering the room. I was their voice and they were invited when I spoke.

"This has never happened," the director said. "What should we do about it?"

"I'll pray," I said. "Will you join me?"

I asked Heavenly Father to help the equipment work. I asked for all of those involved in the filming to feel the love that was here with us as the angel children were present. Most importantly, I asked that the electricity would work so we could conduct the interview.

Within a minute or so of praying, everything came back on. The crew was subdued and worked with greater feelings of reverence than normal.

During the filming I shared an experience our daughter Laura had concerning her brother Matthew before he was born. During my pregnancy with Matthew, Laura, a 10-year-old girl, had seen him standing near Brent one evening during family prayer.

"We'd like to interview your daughter Laura too," the director said.

"I can't call her," I replied. "She's on a mission for our church in Salt Lake City. Unless there is an emergency, I can only contact her through letters."

"We will be in Salt Lake tomorrow interviewing someone else for your segment. If there is any way you can get ahold of Laura, let us know."

As they packed up to leave, I gave them each a copy of *Coming from the Light*. The next day I received an unexpected call from Laura. It had been six months since our last talk.

"Hi Mom," She said. "Is everything okay? I felt there was some reason I needed to call you. I requested and received permission from my mission president."

With the mission president's consent, I contacted the film director with information on how to meet with and film Laura the following day so she could tell them how she saw her brother before he was born. They met with Laura and she shared with them her memory of seeing her unborn brother:

We were having prayer together as a family. During the prayer I opened my eyes and looked up. I saw a man about six feet two inches tall with blond hair and smooth olive skin. His spirit was pure and loving. He was dressed in white attire with a V neck. He had a broad chest and shoulders. He had bare feet and bare forearms. His hands were on the shoulders of my kneeling father. As I gazed at him, I knew I had known and loved him forever. He was my brother Matthew.

A few weeks later one of the camera crew from that show called me. "I am so amazed at the message of your book," he said. "Am I really a child of God?"

Such a simple message was foreign to this man. I was always humbled when others learned this concept for the first time. I repeated how the spirits of children are waiting to come to earth and reassured him yes, he absolutely was a child of God, sent to this earth with a mission to love and serve his fellowman.

"The experience in your home and reading your book has been life changing for me," he said.

Sightings

At that time, *Sightings* was a very popular television show. On three different occasions, I received phone calls from the producer Ruth Raffidi and at her request, shared new stories with her. We became good friends. The show would recreate stories from the books and dramatize them for television.

One of the most moving stories they recreated was that of a little girl named Sarah who had been kidnapped. I met Sarah's family while interviewing them for an article I was writing for *Salt Lake City Deseret News*. Little did I know the horrific experience of being kidnapped included one of the sweetest prebirth experiences I had ever heard, but it took awhile for the story to come to light. Three-year-old Sarah was kidnapped, assaulted and then dumped in the desert, where she stayed for three days, waiting for help. But little Sarah was not alone. An angel—who she said looked just like her sister Heather, stayed by her side. This angel showed Sarah where to wait for help; under the branches of a desert tree. Sarah stayed warm and dry under the tree during an October monsoon downpour. In the morning of the third day, the angel told Sarah to leave the tree and walk in a certain direction. Sarah followed the angel and was soon spotted by a quail hunter and quickly taken to the hospital. Sarah was in shock and didn't speak for a time, but the first thing she said was "I saw Heather playing."

Her parent's knew this was impossible. There was no way Heather could have been there, as she had been in their care the entire time. The most important thing was that Sarah was found and alive.

I documented Sarah's account and remained friends with her family. A few years later, after Sarah's mother had another baby named Jessica, they realized who had been with Sarah in the desert. When Jessica was a little blonde-haired toddler and Sarah was five years old, Sarah said, "It was Jessica who was with me in the desert."

Sarah's guardian angel in the desert was her unborn sister, Jessica.

The accounts of unborn children acting as guardian angels were growing in my files. People were learning the very sacred nature of life through these personal testimonies and I was pleased.

Messages and Miracles

Things were moving along. I had a New York publishing house with an editor who believed in me and who was doing everything he could to get more press for my anticipated best-seller. I was invited back to the Learning Annex to speak again. During my presentation the door opened and a lady poked her head in the room. She asked, "Is this the class on life after death?"

"Well, kind of," I responded and motioned for her to come in and join us. Her eyes were red and her face was flushed. It was obvious she'd been crying and was emotionally very upset. We were about to learn how upset. As she moved to take a seat she announced, "I have come here to this class to see whether I should live or end my life."

As you might imagine, the whole temperament of the class shifted. Hoping to help this woman whom I considered to be my sister in the family of God, I shifted from lecture mode to therapy mode. I asked the group to arrange their seats in a circle. We began asking the distraught woman what was happening in her life. The group was very supportive, giving examples of how they had overcome similar problems.

I interjected comments that my research proved we are children of God who come to earth with a purpose under his guidance. He loves us and when our missions are complete here, He wants us to return to Him, but not on our timing, on his time. Suicide is never the answer.

By the time the class was over the woman was much calmer and there was hope in her voice and in her countenance. There was even a lady who knew the woman's brother and offered to go with her to arrange family support and prevent possible tragedy.

Why had the woman chosen my class that day? I believe she was guided there so that we could help her learn life's enhancing principles.

Opportunities to speak continued. After one lecture, a man on crutches walked toward me with his wife. She was carrying a copy of *Coming from the Light* and said, "I have a chronic illness. When I have this book with me—my pain is less. I sleep with it in my bed—I even take it when I go out—I have experimented with it and your book has an energy that greatly lessens my pain.

Stories like this were amazing. I would have gone on lecturing and seeking media opportunities, but things slowed down. Oprah never called, nor did Geraldo. *Coming from the* Light did not become a best-seller as expected, although it continued to sell consistently and Simon and Schuster kept it in print for over six years. Even though it did not reach great multitudes as hoped, stories as reported above clearly indicate the book had a positive life-changing impact on some people.

It reminded me of the Savior's Parable of the Lost Sheep— saving one at a time is important.

Hay House Documentary

Elliot Rosen, a social worker in California called. He'd received a grant from Louise Hay's Hay House Foundation to produce a film documentary entitled *The Eternal Soul.* He had picked up *Coming from the Light* in a local book store and was thrilled to find the documentation it provided on the eternal nature of the soul. His own research likewise demonstrated that our souls live before we come to earth and Elliot wanted to include our research in his documentary.

Earlier, Brent, who was becoming increasingly involved in my research and writing, offered me a gift for our June 3rd wedding anniversary. With his Ph.D. training in analyzing data, he hung out in our home office and for four days I hardly saw him. He came out only for food, sleep and bathroom breaks.

For 96 hours he reviewed in great detail a sample of 57 prebirth experiences from my files. Just as researchers have identified traits of a typical near death experience, Brent identified traits of a typical prebirth experience. He identified the when, how and to whom and compared the near-death studies to the pre-birth studies.

Elliot was very impressed with this analysis and wanted Brent and I to share our research in his documentary. We scheduled a time, loaded up our kids, drove six hours to California and met Elliot in a beautiful home near the Pacific Ocean. He had a room set up like a film studio. We spent the afternoon filming and talking about the eternal nature of the soul.

The next day we took the kids to Disneyland and had a wonderful time. It's interesting, understanding children come from God and applying it to those children in your life. My children are the light of my life and it is a privilege to be their mother. When I mother, I'm not always thinking about eternal things. If anything, my research teaches me to be in the now. I realize what a small world it is and how quickly time goes by. I cherish my children's faces, and now my grandchildren, their laughter and moments of joy. I want to relish the love of family. Each child has a piece of heaven with them as a distinct part of their personality and talents.

I believe young children instinctively know they are special. They not only want to be watched and praised, but they want to be held and nurtured. A natural side affect of collecting stories about heaven is to aspire to love in as many ways as possible. If we really understand our children, who they are and where they come from, and apply this knowledge in our behavior, then so many things would be different in the world.

Striving to do Good

Many times Brent and I talked about the work it took to do what we were doing. Balancing parenting and marketing a book wasn't easy. Our children had made sacrifices while I was either writing or promoting a book. Brent had worked hard to keep us financially afloat. With my degree in elementary education, I knew I could go back to teaching. The extra income would make a big impact in our family expenses, but I couldn't deny what I was supposed to do.

First and foremost, I was a full-time mother and second, I would do everything I could to share what I knew about our heritage as children of God. I had been from one end of the country to the other. I had done hundreds of phone interviews, radio and television shows, and written for countless hours. Writers block was never a problem because I was fed with beautiful prebirth stories from all over the world. My objective was to share the simplicity of the message: that we come from God.

Sometimes, however, the pressure was too much. There were so many people searching for hope and running from painful pasts. I worried about every abused child I saw on the news. I considered how many abortions were performed each day. I thought of the starving children in war-torn countries around the world. There were days I insisted on carrying the burden, even though I knew it was up to Christ. At times I felt the overwhelming privilege of raising my children in a home with enough food and modern-day comforts. Why wasn't life fair?

Brent reminded me, "Remember Sarah, if you can make a difference in one life, helping one mother recognize the gift of being a mother, helping someone who's miscarried find peace knowing their baby is alright, or helping someone avoid the trauma of abortion for both herself and her child, then it's all worth it."

I had produced and promoted the messages of *Life before Life* and *Coming from the Light* in every way I knew how and I felt it was pleasing to the Lord, but I was running the race in a sprint instead of pacing myself. I knew Brent was right. My job as an author was to teach people through love and understanding. It was not to crush me. It was not to leave me discouraged. I needed to be patient with myself. I worked for God and if He wanted to extend the reach of my work, I knew He would. Otherwise, I was content to do what I could and leave the rest to Him.

Ned Sees His Aborted Children

In the summer of 1995, Brent and I spoke at the University of Hartford in Connecticut at the International Association for Near Death Studies (IANDS) world conference. We presented our research on the relationship between prebirth experiences and near death experiences. We were also eager to learn from other presenters. We attended the lecture of Ned Daughtery and I was totally mesmerized by the things he was shown in heaven during an extensive near death experience. In his own words and from his book, *Fast Lane to Heaven*:

I was neither agnostic nor an atheist—I was too busy being hedonistic and materialistic as a nightclub owner to be bothered with such things. All that changed on a hot July night in 1984. In a moment of rage, I attacked and tried to strangle a business associate. All of a sudden I was the one who could not breathe! I felt my lungs collapse and my heart stop beating before falling into a state of unconsciousness.

The next thing I knew, I was in an ambulance and heard a paramedic say, "I have no vitals—we're losing him!"

I floated out of my human body and out of the ambulance. I hovered over a roadway, watching the last of red tail light tracers as the ambulance disappeared. I felt myself rising into the star-filled sky. Suddenly I knew, "I'm going home!"

At that moment—free of my earthly bondage—I remembered! I had been in the world of spirits before—before I was born.

With this realization I found myself in the presence of a beautiful, radiant and angelic being. She became known to me as the Lady of Light. At one point, she showed me a small group of toddler-aged children who were playing in a heavenly garden.

I particularly noticed two of the children who were to the right of the group. They drew my attention because they had turned and were looking at me. Although I perceived that one was a boy and the other a girl, I was more observant of their identical appearances. Later on, I understood they were twins.

There were several more toddlers playing in the group. As I focused my attention on each of them, they looked directly and longingly toward me, as if they were seeking some acknowledgment or understanding from me. I perceived that I should know these children, but I was confused.

I conveyed to the Lady of Light my need to understand what I should know about the scene before me. She responded by introducing me into yet another scene.

Now I stood at an academic campus on a sunny and glorious day with a group of people I did not immediately recognize, except for a handsome young man dressed in a cap and gown. I was filled with love, joy and pride for the young man celebrating his graduation.

I was perplexed by my reaction to the young man at his graduation. During that moment I experienced emotions that I had never known before, emotions that only a proud father could know, but I never wanted to be a father.

Then I was back in the heavenly garden, filled with even more questions. I wanted to know the meaning of these visions. I did not have any children, nor did I plan on having any. Up to that moment, I had thought of kids as an inconvenience and a nuisance that had no place in my life.

The prospect of such a long-term commitment as fatherhood was frightening to me. As I meditated over what I was seeing, the group of children slowly vanished, disappearing from before my eyes. I felt an excruciating loss, a terrible, heart-wrenching and aching pain.

I was feeling the loss of these children.

Then I realized who they were. During my life, opportunities to have children were given me on several occasions, but I had chosen against them. When the women in my life became pregnant, I insisted that they have abortions.

Now I saw that these children were not "choices!" I realized that they were the spirits of children who were intended to be mine during my earth life. They were opportunities I had decided were inconveniences. I pondered the scene before me, now absent the children, for what seemed a long period of time. Then a small boy appeared in the garden from the direction where the Lady of Light stood. He was very strong

and full of life. He had blond hair and big blue eyes.

I turned to the Lady of Light, whom I recognized was Mary, the mother of Jesus. I conveyed to her that I wanted to know who this little boy was, and the significance of the scene before me. I still didn't anticipate having children. Was this little boy to be my son?

She responded, "Truly, he is a son of God!"

Suddenly I was sent back to my body. I didn't want to be here, but God didn't want me up there either. And it was His decision, not mine.

As I came back from death, I was told I was sent back with a mission in this life. I didn't know what it was at first, but I now find that each and every day it is defined for me a little more clearly. I know that I have a destiny.

Some time later, on April 7, 1991, I became a father. My son's name is Michael Christopher, after his grandpa and after the Archangel Michael.

Michael had blond hair that was almost golden and, the biggest blue eyes I have ever seen on a little boy.

He's the luckiest little boy in the world, because I am a great daddy!

I was present in the delivery room when Michael came into this world. What an experience it was! What a miracle! The miracle of life! I watched Michael being born and his strong little body struggle as he took his first breath. I felt a life force of energy fill the delivery room, and a rush of wind rolled by my ears carrying a message. It was the message I remembered from before: "Truly, he is a son of God!"

My mind was racing. This was the first time I heard about another person with a memory of children they had aborted. More and more, I was beginning to understand, at least to a small degree, what may happen to aborted children. I never accepted the world's belief that they no longer exist. I knew they were eternal souls. But here was a person who had actually seen in a near death experience their aborted children. These angel children remembered the parent who rejected them. I wanted to know more.

What were their options now? Could they come again? Could they be reassigned to other parents who would want them? When they came back did subconscious memories of being aborted affect their lives on earth? Did they bring any of the traumas of being aborted with them? These were questions I wanted to answer through more research. If Ned had a memory of aborted children, certainly other people would too. I prayed I could find them and learn more.

Was I a Guardian Angel Before I was Born?

On the way back from Connecticut, Brent and I visited my parents in Eastern Tennessee for a week. It was not an easy time. My dad was sick with lung cancer. His time was confined to the family room recliner, the restful front porch couch, or his bed. Conversation was tempered by his shortness of breath, yet in Dad's self-effacing way, it was he who tried to comfort us. I asked about his childhood and wrote careful notes on what he told me. In the past he seemed to reflect a lot on life and didn't normally say much. My dad was a quiet gentleman, but at this moment he was ready to talk.

"Our home was on a large hill surrounded by mountains, a big two-story house with a double living room," he said. "I remember the old saying; memories of the elderly seem to be based on childhood. Most of mine are from four to seven years old in the depression area. I was the ninth child born to mother. After World War I, my oldest brother came back from the war with a small specimen bottle with his appendix in formaldehyde. I was told at the age of five the appendix was worth a dollar at a medical school. Money was very scarce at this time and I wondered who I could sell it to.

"My thoughts of my mother are compared to a setting hen. Diligently she watched over her young children. She seemed to be a little partial to her oldest and youngest sons, favoring me with a trip to North Carolina to visit my grandfather. I was about four at this time. Mother was sick a lot, being very thin with severe headaches. She would tie a cloth around her head to relieve the headaches. We had three doctors in our town. Dr. William's diagnosis of mother's condition was cancer of the uterus. At this time, there was not much treatment for cancer in this stage. He suggested and made an appointment for her to go to Philadelphia where they were treating cancer with radium.

"Dr. Jones and Mother rode the train and he stayed with her the entire time as she received several treatments of radium. We knew when she would be returning and we waited for her at the train station in Johnson City. When the train arrived we took Mother across the street and waited in the lobby of a small hotel until time to take her home. She brought me a pear from Philadelphia. She had mashed it a lot and made it very juicy. She told me to give my sister half of it, but being four years of age, I ate it all. She did not make any progress as the radium had burned her so bad that we had to take the webbed seat out of a wooden chair so she could tolerate sitting in it. Her health kept failing and she had such terrible pain she would constantly take morphine that she had in a little black pill can. The pain persisted on and on. The pain was so bad when night came she would go to her room and get down on her knees and pray to die.

"On November 24, 1924, she seemed to go into a coma. The children thought she was dead and they began to cry. They aroused her for a few minutes. The children were told to leave the room and close the door. In a few more minutes, she was dead. At this time I was playing in the front yard. When I heard the crying, as a five year old, I knew she was dead. My mother was buried on Thanksgiving Day in Hall Cemetery with one small bunch of artificial flowers.

"As many difficulties and problems that have been part of my life, I know she has watched over me thru sickness and war. I have been blessed with her love and memories."

My father had never before spoken of such things. His words gave me comfort and cushioned the fall of knowing he would soon die.

Later, my mother and I were sitting in the front yard under the shade of the old maple tree. As I had done many times, I asked questions about my dad's mom, Grandmother Naoma.

As a young girl, I frequently picked up my Grandma Naoma's small framed photograph and gazed into her dark eyes. Out of my two grandmothers, she was the one I felt closest to, yet she died long before I was born. How could she be so familiar to me? It was puzzling because I had never met her.

That day I shared with Mom one of my childhood memories. One time while visiting my Aunt Jo, I went to look at my favorite picture of Grandma Naoma but it was no longer on the table where it usually was.

"Where is the picture of my Grandma?" I asked. "Can you let me see it?"

Aunt Jo found it in the back of the cabinet and let me hold it again. I was content.

During my visit, Mom told me Grandma Naoma was only 47 years old when she died.

"Why would no one in the family ever speak about her?" I asked. "Why would they change the subject, or leave upset if anyone mentioned her name?"

That day, without explanation, Mother seemed open to discussing the events of Grandma Naoma's life. Maybe it was because my dad was ill and we had so little time left. I listened in silence, not wanting to disturb what was being said. Mom told me terrible things that happened to my grandmother, things I had never heard—violent and abusive acts inflicted upon her.

Suddenly—in a flash—I saw myself as a spirit person dressed in white. I knew it was before I was born. I was standing in my grandmother's bedroom in front of an old grandfather clock. My heart felt of her pain and I offered what comfort I could. I believe I was acting in the role of her guardian angel, but in God's wisdom I was not allowed to intervene at that time.

I was there, I think, to witness the violence inflicted upon her so I might testify at some future time concerning what had happened. As the scene closed, I knew that I had been with her in various episodes of her life on this earth. That day visiting with my mother helped me to finally understand that my love for Grandma Naoma stemmed from my spirit's memory of being with her before I was born.

I have felt Grandmother Naoma with me many times throughout my life. One such incident happened when I was home taking care of my infant daughter, Sarah Rebekah. Suddenly I felt Naoma's presence there with me, watching me as I loved and cared for my child. I felt the love she had for me and my family. Her presence was comforting. The thought came to me that we had taken on similar roles in the spirit world, watching over one another. I believe we have an eternal bond that goes back a very long time.

Time raced by and too soon we had to leave for the airport. Dad, with Mom at his side, bravely made it to the front porch for tearful goodbye hugs. As the car eased north through the shade tunnel of poplars and elms, Dad waved and smiled stoically from that porch of memories, a haven of refreshing evening breezes and cherished visits with relatives and neighbors.

It was the last time I saw my father alive.

In October, the hospital became Dad's home. He asked that I not return until the funeral. Our summer visit was the memory he treasured, and he didn't want me to see him as an invalid. I honored his request. My sister Sandra came from her home in Seattle, Washington, and served as a loving caregiver for Mom and Dad through this trying time.

One day in Arizona I felt Dad's mother Naoma draw near with a message, "Your prayers have been heard and granted. Your father has only a few days left on the earth. When he passes over, I promise I will be there to greet him."

I had prayed often that his mother would come for him when it was his time to pass, knowing how much it would mean to him.

Later, Mom called, upset and crying. "Dad is losing it," she said. "He's talking to people no one else can see. He looks at the ceiling and talks to his brother who's been dead for years. He points to the wall and describes a beautiful place where he's going. He insists I take him home to pack his luggage. I can't stand to see him this way."

I had learned those who are dying will often leave final gifts for their family; gifts of seeing family members from the other side, gifts of forgiveness, gifts of love expressed that was not previously spoken, and so on.

"Mom, Dad's not losing it," I said. "His loved ones are coming to greet him. He sees parts of heaven where he is going. He's trying to share his experiences with you. All you need to do is acknowledge what he says and accept it."

I knew that hospice nurses hear these kinds of things all the time as a patient approaches death. Actually, these are positive signs.

In Dad's case what was more amazing was that until now, he had never believed in heaven and now he was seeing it. Although he attended church with us, he never discussed how he felt about anything spiritual or religious. He never offered prayer. Mom had always been the spiritual one. She believed my explanation and was comforted by my words.

The following day, Dad was gone.

Roy Mills—A Friend from Heaven

The summer of 1995 was a season of highs and lows.

After seeing my father for the last time, it was with heavy hearts that Brent and I embarked on the last stage of our trip before returning to our Arizona home. We flew to Georgia to meet Roy Mills and his wife, Phyllis. We had been phone friends for about a year ever since a publisher we worked with had called and said, "We received a letter from a fellow in Georgia who claims to have memories of his life in heaven before coming to earth. Isn't that the area you are researching? Would you call him and see what he wants?"

I called Roy and over the weeks we visited, I found Roy's story so intriguing that Brent and I agreed to help him write a book about it. After a year of interviews, we were about to have the privilege of spending three days with Roy and Phyllis in person.

Roy had never sent us a picture of himself. For some reason I had envisioned him as a tall masculine fellow so you can imagine my shock when we exchanged descriptions of whom to look for at the airport and he described himself as 4 foot 10 inches tall and weighing 350 pounds.

"My goodness," I thought to myself, "He is a cube, almost as wide as he is tall!"

We flew into Tallahassee, Florida, the nearest major airport to Roy's home in Bainbridge, Georgia. We entered the terminal and scanned the crowd looking for a "cube." We didn't see anyone who met this description, but we kept looking, thinking, "Maybe he's too short to be seen in a crowd."

At the same time, my eyes were drawn to a tall burly fellow wearing a red baseball cap leaning against a wall. As we walked closer, I could see he was crying. He broke into a big grin and extended his hand while wiping his eyes with a handkerchief, "Hey Sarah, I'm Roy."

So "the cube" was a joke, one of many we would come to enjoy from this delightful man. Brent and I hugged Roy like old friends and Roy said to me, "I'm crying because I remember you from heaven."

We gathered our luggage and Roy led us out to his car to meet Phyllis. She had not come into the terminal with Roy due to her delicate health. As a young woman she had been an athletic "tom- boy." Now she wore a shoulder strap bag that provided a 24-7 medicinal drip into her stomach. There were days when she was too weak and in pain to leave home, but on this day she'd made the effort and was excited to meet us. We were touched.

Soon we passed Roy's worksite, a plywood plant in Florida where he repaired machines, one of which had nearly chewed off his hand—but that's a miraculous story for another time. When we crossed the border into Georgia, Roy said, "I like to tell people I have an important executive job that requires me to travel and work out of state frequently."

In about an hour we checked in at the motel in Bainbridge. Then Roy and Phyllis treated us to a luscious southern buffet— fried okra, collard greens, pinto bean soup, biscuits and gravy, fried chicken, all the southern foods I love. We ate there three days in a row. It was so good I predicted if we ate there much longer, we'd all be "cubes."

For three days we thoroughly enjoyed the company of Roy and Phyllis . . . they were living testimony to "southern hospitality." He told us that in the pre-existence all of nature, such as flowers, grass, trees, hills, and water, radiates light and intelligence. The variety and brilliance of colors is beyond mortal imagination. Roy also recalls buildings, classrooms, auditoriums, teachers, instructors and tutors in a celestial education system that prepares each soul to come to earth. When, as an unborn spirit, he reached a certain level of preparation, he remembers being taught about earth trials and tests. He learned how he could progress personally through challenges and how he could help others. Then came a time when he actually participated in choosing his future life tests on earth. Roy was so excited about this process that he initially chose five difficult earth tests. The supervising angels intervened, explaining they appreciated his enthusiasm, but that he had chosen more challenges than were realistic. He had to "put two back," so to speak.

Roy recalls a gathering in a large auditorium with many "little spirits," as he referred to himself and other souls at that stage. It might be compared to a graduation ceremony where our Heavenly Father was present to confirm final approval of each soul's earth mission. Roy noted that although some missions are great and others are small by earth standards, in heaven all missions are considered great. There was no jealousy there, only cheering and support for each soul as their earth missions were assigned.

Just before Roy left this heavenly place to be born, he met and was blessed by Jesus. Soon thereafter, Roy was taken to a "departure room" where several of his closest teachers embraced him in loving farewells. He was introduced to his escort angel who brought him to earth where his spirit entered the tiny body his mother was preparing for him in her womb.

Roy's prebirth memories give him a unique perspective on the purpose of earth life. He said, *"We come to live in the physical world so that we can grow spiritually by gaining experience and exercising our free will. Many of those experiences involve hardships which can only happen on earth, because heaven is a place of perfect love, forgiveness, peace and tranquility. These hardships are necessary to help us build faith and exercise the gifts God has given us. Each of us is given a mission to accomplish while we are here, but we are allowed to select some of the challenges that will bring us growth.*

"The angels help us choose our experiences, because what we choose must fit with our mission and with God's overall plan for our lives. Some people choose a life of extreme sacrifices or nearly unbearable suffering. The light of God shines brightly around these people and in Heaven they are thought of as mighty spirits, because they come to earth to suffer so that others can grow in understanding and love."

Roy developed relationships with his future children before he was prepared to leave heaven and be born on earth:

"I remember the first time I met my children in Heaven. My angel guide had taken me to a room with a lot of seats, like an auditorium. She had me sit near the front and told me to face forward and not turn around. Then she left. Soon, I heard giggling coming from behind me and when I turned around to see who was making the sound, I saw three little spirits like me. I started talking to these young spirits, communicating by a type of telepathy, and we shared a great deal of information at a tremendous speed. Before long, I discovered that they were going to be my sons on earth. I thought that was amazing, because they appeared to be the same "age" in the spirit world as me."

Roy believes that the remembrance of God's plan has guided him through his life experiences.

We listened intently to Roy's life story, including his memories of our pre-earth life in heaven and his near-death experience in which he returned briefly to heaven as a boy. He also told us how he came to be raised by his grandparents near swamps with alligators and cottonmouth snakes, and how he met and married Phyllis. As Roy drove us down country dirt roads and showed us where various events occurred, we took detailed notes, laughed and cried and enjoyed every minute with him.

At dinner the first night, Roy explained why he cried upon seeing me at the airport. "Sarah, when I saw you I had a flashback— you were one of my best friends in heaven. I remember you as a little blond girl. Our missions here are similar. Yours is to help the little ones come and to teach others that we live with God before we are born. There is a real crisis now in heaven concerning the little ones making it to earth."

During our three days with Roy, we came to know him as an honest, spiritual and good man. We believe his memories to be true. As to his goodness, you've never seen anyone kinder or more solicitous than Roy was to his invalid wife. It was remarkable the way he cared for her both physically and emotionally. Phyllis has passed on now, surely to a greater reward. Because of her noble suffering, Roy saw Phyllis as a "mighty spirit" in the eternal scheme.

A Birthday Gift for Mom

A year after my father died, Mom asked me to visit her in Tennessee for her 75th birthday. She felt impressed that this would be a very special birthday for her and wanted me to be with her. Mom was doing well in many ways, but she missed dad. They had a great love affair for over fifty years.

I decided to accept Mom's invitation and fly to Tennessee for her birthday. I had not been home since my Dad's funeral the previous November. It was hard to be home in the old house where I had grown up. The absence of dad in the home was ever present for me. I would turn in the hallway and expect to see him. He used to whistle while working in the yard or pulling weeds in the garden. What I would give to hear the old tunes he used to hum under his breath. But I was determined to be cheerful, at least for Mom's sake, and see that she had a wonderful birthday.

We celebrated with friends and family on Saturday. On Sunday morning, I told Mom that I wanted to drive over to the little LDS chapel for Sabbath day services. Mom was not a member of the LDS church and declined my invitation to attend with me.

I was especially happy that morning for some reason. The fall leaves were ablaze in gold and red and crunched beneath my feet as I walked to the car. I drove my parents' car through the tree lined streets to the chapel. I noticed a tape in the car tape player and pulled it out. It was a Glenn Miller special, the only tape that my dad had ever purchased. I put it in and soon the music of Glenn Miller, Dad's favorite, was playing in the car.

It wasn't surprising that I began to feel very emotional. Tears filled my eyes. Was I simply feeling nostalgic, missing Dad? Something felt different. Then it hit me—my dad was sitting in the front seat of the car next to me.

Feeling his presence was a beautiful experience I was not prepared for. Tears began to flow—fast and full. I pulled two tissues from my purse to wipe away the tears. By the time I reached the chapel, the tissues were a wet ball in my hand.

I sat in the parking lot trying to understand this experience. I have learned that when someone comes from the other side, I need to take the time to be quiet and meditate upon it. There is always a message to be delivered. I took out my journal that I had been impressed to bring to take notes during church. I sat, listened. My dad was speaking to me and I began to write.

"Sarah, I am here with you. Your prayers for me that I would find Christ have been heard. I did not understand when I lived on the earth. When you tried to teach me about God, I was afraid. Now I want us to be an eternal family."

Something I had never imagined was happening on this special day. My father was talking to me about Jesus.

I stayed in the car for a few more moments, then proceeded into the church and found a seat in the back of the chapel. Dad was still with me. It was a holy time as I listened to the words of the speakers and for the first time— with my dad by my side. I continued to write impressions from him as I sat there. What came was a sweet love letter from dad for me to give to mom!

Then there was one final thought from him: *"Sarah, go home and tell your mom what has happened. I will go with you. I want you to tell your mother that Christ lives."*

This had become a very emotional day for me. And now, Dad wanted me to go home and tell these things to my mother? Would she understand that Dad was with me?

I cried all the way home. When I opened the front door, Mom was sitting in the living room waiting for me. I ran to her and said "Mom, you won't believe me when I tell you what has happened."

"Tell me!" she said.

I told her everything and she was so happy. It was her greatest dream to know her husband lived, even after death. She had always believed in Christ and now, to think her sweetheart was with Him.

We both cried and hugged one another.

"I told you that this would be a special birthday," she said with tears in her eyes.

Speaking on Capitol Hill

It was 1997 and I had impressions I should go to Washington D.C. during the partial birth abortion hearings, following which Congress would vote regarding the legality of this horrendous "medical procedure."

Partial birth abortion was a new term, although not a new procedure. The public was not aware that these types of abortions were taking place, let alone legal. Many in Congress wanted to ban this "frankensteinian" procedure. Partial birth abortion takes place when a woman is in her third trimester and the baby is viable.

In other words, the baby could be born premature and survive, but is aborted before taking its first breath. The mother is fully dilated, the baby's head crowns when the abortion doctor inserts a sharp scissor-like instrument through the soft spot into the infant's brain, killing the baby before it ever has a chance to let out its first cry. As long as the baby has a foot still inside the mother, "it is not born" and the procedure is legal. If the baby is outside the mother, the procedure is murder.

Once again money was tight, but Brent supported me. With careful budgeting, we found a way to pay for the flight. I knew this wasn't a time to sit and watch history take place around me. I needed to be bold and I would do it. I wanted to share my books with law makers on Capitol Hill. I contacted my Congressman, with whom I was acquainted, and told him I wanted to share my research with him and others. He was familiar with my books and agreed that it was a good idea.

I scheduled my trip and once in D.C., stood in line until I was finally allowed entry to listen to the debates by United States Congressmen and Senators. Standing in line, there were people around me screaming and yelling, "Don't stop partial birth abortion.

It is a women's right to choose." I remember thinking, "It feels like a hole has been punched in the wall of hell and these people came out to fight for the right to kill innocent children."

Once inside the building, I saw one of the most valiant of all warriors for the unborn, Henry Hyde, a U.S Senator from Illinois. He walked past me, not knowing who I was. I handed him a card I had prepared before I left home with a quote I had written down that he had previously said, to perhaps use in my talk:

When the time comes as it surely will, when we face that terrible moment, the final judgment, I've often thought as Cardinal Fulton Sheen wrote, that it is a terrible moment of loneliness. You have no advocates there, you are there alone standing before God, and a terror will rip your soul like nothing you can imagine. [By contrast], I really think that those in the pro-life movement will not be alone. I think there will be a chorus of voices that have never been heard in this world but are heard very beautifully and very loudly in the next world and I think they will plead for everyone who has been in the [pro-life] movement.

They [the aborted] will say to God, "Spare them, because they loved us." And God will look at us and ask not, "Did you succeed?" but "Did you try?"

Henry Hyde, a mighty and valiant voice, spoke eloquently and emotionally about why partial-birth abortion should be outlawed. People in the audience were moved to tears. Voting wouldn't take place for days, so I walked the halls of the congressional building, hoping to speak with anyone I could influence. I stopped Rick Santorum and handed him my book. He thanked me for what I was doing and explained, "My wife wrote a book about our baby that died and what that baby taught us about the sanctity of life."

I handed out at least fifty books that day, mostly to interns who worked for congressmen and senators.

My congressman arranged for me to speak at a caucus meeting in which researchers like me could share their latest findings. Reality set in. What was I thinking? Could I really do this? I found courage in the right to life messages of others who had spoken earlier. Several congressmen sent their aides and I spoke to a group of people in a room in the Rayburn Building on Capitol Hill. After introducing myself, I shared the following message:

Only heaven has a precise count of the total number of children aborted and castaway from earth. Surely the number has increased by millions in the last half of the 20th Century. We live in a day when astronomical numbers are heard so often as to dull their significance. Remember, each abortion is not just a statistic, but an individual experience—each individual is torn from the womb by sharp instruments or burned by caustic solutions, rejected and sent back to heaven one at a time. I would like to share a story given to me by a woman that demonstrates the sanctity of life and the Life Giver.

I was five and a half months pregnant with my third child. The doctors discovered I had gallstones blocking my bile duct. With immediate surgery the doctors saved my life and I was out of danger. The surgery took many hours and was very difficult. I bled heavily, and for a few seconds my heart stopped. My husband was told there was little chance the baby would survive.

One difficult night after the surgery, the nurse was performing a routine check of the baby's heartbeat. She could not find it. She checked for over half an hour and finally called a nurse and doctor from the maternity floor. They checked for over an hour. I was told that they felt the baby had died, and they started to set up an ultrasound to verify it. They left to call my husband and my doctor.

Alone in the darkened hospital room, I poured out my heart to the Lord. My heart grieved for the baby I had never held, the smiles I had never seen, the steps never carefully counted. As I plead with the Lord for strength and peace for my spirit, I fell into a deep sleep.

I dreamt that I was at the bottom of a flight of white steps. Around me was my husband, two sons, parents, sister, brother, and departed loved ones. I heard my name called and looked up to the top of the staircase. There was a throne surrounded by a light and a figure standing before the throne. A feeling of great love, compassion, warmth, and calmness entered my spirit. I climbed the stairs and knelt on the step below his feet. I bowed my head in reverence and awe. Suddenly hands descended into my view. In these beautiful hands rested a shining baby wrapped in white. I gazed into crystal blue eyes with beautiful black lashes. She had dark black hair, and she smiled at me. I began to cry from joy and amazement.

Then I heard these words, "I give this child to you to raise for me. She is a gift that someday you will return to me. She is my little sister and is very beloved. Teach her of my love. Show her my example. Help her find me and my path. I died for her and for the chance to bring her back to Father. Behold the precious gift I give to you."

The light grew and suddenly I knew her. I received glimpses of long ago and promises made. I yearned to keep those promises and to hold my precious gift.

The bundle was placed in my hands, and my tears dropped to the white blanket. I felt awed and amazed at this great trust in me. How could I ever be worthy of this beautiful girl? I slowly walked down the stairs and stood before my husband. I held out my arms, and he gently took the angel of light from me.

I suddenly awoke when the doctor returned. I told him to check the baby again, because I knew she was alive and strong. He agreed and on his first try found a strong, regular heartbeat.

Three months later I gave birth to a seven-pound six-ounce baby girl. She had crystal blue eyes, dark black hair, and looked exactly like the baby in my dream.

As I gazed into her eyes, I saw again my angel wrapped in light. The heartfelt prayer of a mother "availeth much." Her prayer,

thankfully, was answered positively, and her child was saved.

I spoke a few words, and then went back to my seat. It took most of the evening for my hands to stop shaking. A few weeks later home in my living room I heard the heart breaking news. Partial birth abortion had **not** been banned.

Congress had passed the act and now it was up to individual states to determine if they would allow partial birth abortions to remain legal. The fight to save the unborn would go on and I would be there, if possible.

A State's Right to Choose

Several months later, another opportunity arose for me to speak and defend the rights of the unborn. I was invited by my friend, Congresswoman Karen Johnson, to speak at a breakfast of legislators, business, and professional leaders from the greater Phoenix area. Motivated by my love for children, including the unborn, I prepared my speech diligently and prayerfully to fit the half-hour time frame I was promised. There was a sense of urgency in the air. Partial-birth abortion laws were under debate in the Arizona legislature. The people at this lecture could influence the final vote.

The morning of the breakfast, the speaker scheduled for the first half-hour went on and on, taking most of my time. When I was finally introduced, only seven minutes remained before the meeting's end. My fully prepared speech was out of the question. On the short walk to the podium, I silently prayed for guidance on what to say that would make a difference in so short a span.

Looking out over the audience, I set my notes aside and was determined to speak from my heart. First, I quickly explained my research on the unborn, sharing briefly some of the stories I have collected, demonstrating that each soul lives before earth life and has a time, place, and purpose to be born.

Next, I spoke of the Oscar-winning film, *Schindler's List*. Schindler knew about Hitler's insidious plan to destroy the Jews. While most of his fellow countrymen were either ignoring or contributing to the holocaust, Schindler risked his life to protect the rights and lives of Jews. He could not save them all, but he resolved to rescue as many as he could. This courageous man wept over lives he was unable to save. But the fact is Schindler's noble efforts saved many thousands of innocent people.

I continued, "Today there is another group of innocents being systematically destroyed—the unborn. Those of you who protect the lives of the unborn against abortion, you are Schindler's. Each soul you save makes a difference."

I concluded with this account from our files:

A young boy drowned and later revived. After he had recovered, he described to his mother the brother he had met during his near death experience. Puzzled, the mother reminded her son, "Honey, you know you don't have a brother."

"Yes I do, Mommy. He was pulled from your tummy when you were only fourteen."

The mother was stunned. It was true. She had become pregnant at fourteen and secretly had the child aborted. She never told a living soul—not her husband, not even her parents.

My time was up. A gentle silence hung over the room. Eyes were moist. They had heard the message, that our brothers and sisters were entitled to their birthright on earth, the same as we who have already come.

A few days after my talk, the Arizona State Legislature voted to ban partial birth abortion. The Congresswoman called and explained that a week earlier there were not enough votes to ban partial birth abortion. She said, "Of those who voted to protect the innocent, many had heard, or heard about your seven-minute talk one morning that changed hearts toward unborn children. It was your message, Sarah that did it!"

I thanked her, hung up the phone and returned to washing dishes. I looked the same on the outside, but on the inside I was stunned. I think I was in shock. The next day, I sat on the couch trying to remember clearly what had happened. I picked up the phone and called Karen's office back,

Congresswoman Johnson answered the phone.

"Did you call me yesterday and tell me partial birth abortion has been banned in Arizona?" I said.

"Yes, Sarah, we did it! Not only was it your speech, but I called other legislators who were not there when you spoke and read them stories from your book. I could hear their voices cracking with emotion over the phone. Because of what you had to share, we had enough votes changed so that we could ban partial-birth abortion in Arizona."

I was finally able to absorb what happened and was overcome with joy. The memories and stories of these heavenly children had made a difference.

A Book with Startling New Information

I knew there were various types of prebirth experiences. The most common prebirth experience I had heard about was when an unborn child announces to family members, primarily mothers that they are ready to be born.

These experiences typically come through visions, dreams, hearing a voice, telepathy, a child speaking in your mind or other means of communication, or from different children with different messages. However, a certain file in my drawer was growing faster then the other ones—one called "abortion stories."

My original call to collect stories from others who had seen there unborn children naturally progressed to the point where I was getting stories about aborted children and those who remembered their own abortion. It appeared the stories of the aborted ones were coming to me through heaven's own marketing strategies. I was not soliciting these stories.

Sometimes ideas for a new book are announced to me by something I read, or something said by a friend or even a stranger. In the spring of 1999, I was experiencing this energy—feeling that my next book was on children who'd been aborted. By 1999, a new book began forming in my mind with ideas that flowed so fast I scrambled for a pencil and paper often.

This increased for several weeks as I formulated plans on how to proceed.

I'd been lecturing for ten years on prebirth experiences and the rights of unborn children. Frequently people came up to me afterwards and shared their thoughts. Some of those accounts were about how abortion affected not only women, but the children they chose not too bear. The first story of this nature came to me during the early 1990s. I dismissed it for publishing because it sounded so unbelievable, but now I was hearing more and more stories about how memories of abortion were affecting people.

I needed evidence to answer many specific questions. Does the spirit of a child who is aborted continue to live? If so, do these spirits have opportunity to come to earth again? Do they return to the same parents or are they reassigned to a different family in a sort of Plan B? I absolutely believe that souls are eternal and they are given additional opportunities to be born. Now I needed to gather more evidence.

Willing Mothers

One day my friend Kathy called to tell me about a story she'd found. A woman named Cherie Logan described seeing each of her children in prebirth experiences before they were born. Her first child, a son named Marshall, was born prematurely and lived only two months. Over the years Cherie still ached to hold him and grieved over his welfare. She would ask herself, "What happened to him? Why was his life so short? Where is he? Is he okay?"

Then she wrote:

One day before I was pregnant with my seventh baby, I was sitting with a friend in our living room. Suddenly my friend, in an awed voice said, "Cherie, there are spirits here!" She experienced this right along with me.

My son Marshall came and stood before me. He assured me he was well and happy and I should cease grieving for him. Also in the room were the children I had seen who were waiting to be born. Then Marshall stepped aside and there was standing in front of me a child I had never seen.

This child said, "I beg entry into your family." I agreed instantly as we were always willing to have more children. As if I had never spoken, he again said, "I beg entry into your family." I agreed again, beginning to wonder why the repetition.

A third time he spoke, "I beg entry into your family." This time I spoke in detail. I told him that we would be happy to have him, that we wanted as many children as the Lord would be willing to send us. After that last agreement on my part, as I spoke the words, the heavens opened to me and I saw Jesus Christ standing by a beautiful tree. Then he took me to a field that was full of white cradles. Inside the cradles were babies, many, many, many babies. Some, but not all, of the babies held a piece of paper clutched in their hands.

He said, "These are the cast off ones," meaning those who had been purposely aborted. "My presence is all that keeps their grief from overwhelming them. Their blood cries to me from the earth."

Then, as I looked at the babies and the paper some held in their hands, He said to me, "That paper represents The Willingness of Mothers." It was said as a title. It meant the willingness of any woman to have children, even the ones who could not have children because of illness or age, but who, in their hearts, would have children if they could. Then He said, "It is the willingness of mothers to someday have them that gives them hope."

Suddenly the vision closed, and I again saw the boy in front of me. He said this time, "I am a Cast-off One, and I beg entry into your family."

I said, "Yes." Instantly there appeared in his hand that white paper [apparently a contract guaranteeing he would be born to that "willing mother"].

Then he looked at me and said, "My name is Joshua and I bring with me an extension of your life."

Joshua was now at peace, knowing that I already loved him and would not reject him. His pleadings ceased, he disappeared and I found myself back in my home with my friend. From the details she described as a second witness, I was fortified concerning the validity of the experience.

Then Joshua vanished from my sight, but it did not end with that. When I became pregnant with my seventh child (Ryan), I would frequently see Joshua. Often standing with him was a young woman. One time she informed me that because Joshua was coming to our family, she wanted to come too. She said that where they were, she had been caring for Joshua and she wanted to be in the same family as he so she could continue caring for him.

She is my sweet Cheyanne, who was born after Ryan. I had seen her in vision long before I had seen Joshua. The Lord always knew that I would welcome each little life. I wonder if Joshua will be one of Cheyanne's sons or a precious nephew.

After I read Cherie's story, I emailed her. I introduced myself and told her what an impact her experience had on me. I explained I was working on a book in which I would love to share her story for the benefit of others. She graciously agreed.

The Castaways

One day I was at my holistic doctor's office and overheard two women in conversation. One of them spoke of her near death experience as a child. During her NDE she had seen her unborn children in heaven. Of course, this sparked my attention and I interjected, "I happened to overhear your conversation. I am writing a book. May I hear more of your experience?"

By this time, she was gathering up her purse and preparing to leave. She said, "I don't have time now. I can take your phone number and give you a call. We can get together sometime and talk."

I wrote down my phone number and handed it to her as she went out the door. I should have asked for her number, but she seemed in such a rush.

I was relieved a few days later when Debbie called and agreed to come over that same afternoon. I learned that she'd had an extremely traumatic life. She was abused by age five to the point of death. Her spirit left her body and went to heaven. She was told she needed to return to earth and finish her mission. She resisted going back to the family where she would suffer more abuse. Then she was shown her children. She reacted, "How can I have children? I'm only five!"

"No, they are your future children you will have when you're grown up," her escort explained.

Debbie tried to convince her future children to accept another mother, but they insisted they must be born through her in order to fill their missions. Finally she consented and the Savior himself sent her back to earth with a promise of comfort.

We continued to visit and I told Debbie about some of my experiences and my thoughts on writing a book about abortion. She felt impressed to call another friend of hers, who came over within a short while. As we talked we experienced things only heaven could bring. I was reminded of the scripture, *"Where two or three are gathered in my name, there I will be also."*

We were impressed that, from heaven's perspective, this book would have an important message.

After that day and evening, heaven's influence continued. That night I outlined the book. The title was to be *The Castaways* and was to be a small book with six chapters.

The impression came to me: "It will testify of the innocent children who have been cast away by abortion. It will touch the hearts of women who have had abortions. It will touch the hearts of those considering abortion and their hearts will be changed to give the child life by keeping the baby or adopting it out."

Soon I had written several pages in my journal. I was told a painting of the Savior with a child or children would be given me for the cover. Also, the book needed to be finished and published in the year 2000.

After that experience, I think it was natural for me to wonder, "Why me?" I'm a mother of many children with a busy household to run. All I can say is that the Lord sometimes uses the weak things of the earth to do His work. I admit that I am weak. But I believe that makes me depend on the Lord and his help even more. I believe the Lord is going to bring a flood of light to the world in our day through people who are weak or ordinary, but who seek to do the Lord's will.

A few days later while driving home from work, Brent had such a strong impression to write this book with me that he pulled over to the side of the road and wrote down what he was experiencing.

He had helped me before with analyzing data, but now he felt called to help in writing and interviewing people with stories. I was grateful.

I had continued reassurance that Brent and I would be guided as we wrote *The Castaways*. I remembered a blessing from years earlier when Brent had put his hands on my head and told me, "You will write books that will inspire mothers and fathers to have a family. Your books will soften many hearts toward unborn children. Your books will go out in every form of media—music, film, television, radio, the spoken and the written word. When it comes, it will come with the power to send it forth."

One day when Brent and I were working on *The Castaways*, he called me into his office to read to me what he had written. The beauty of the stories read like poetry and I was carried away in the message. In my mind, I uttered a question: "Did an angel help him write this?"

As instantly as I had the thought, there was Daniel, my son I had miscarried years earlier. He was a being of light; beautiful and holy. He was a tall and slender young man dressed in white, standing behind Brent who was seated at his desk. Daniel's hands were on his father's shoulders. He was looking straight ahead at the computer, as if he were speaking the words while Brent was writing them down.

As I watched Daniel, he turned his head and looked at me. There was a face that had no cares of the world on it, a beautiful face of an eternal spirit. He spoke to me, mind to mind, of the love he had for his dad. It was a humble expression of the love of a son for his father. I was moved to tears, feeling overwhelmed at my love for Daniel and for Brent. And then, to my gaze, Daniel was gone.

She Didn't Understand

Early in the writing of *The Castaways*, I received a startling phone call. A woman on the other end of the phone explained that her deceased sister Susan came to her in a dream and told her to contact Sarah Hinze. The woman had done an internet search and found my contact information. Here is her story as we prepared it for publishing:

Since my sister's passing, I have pieced together her story. The prompting to do so came one night shortly after her death. There Susan was in my dream—so real I felt I could reach out and touch her. She was radiant . . . more at peace than ever I had seen her during earth life. The reason— knowledge.

Susan now understood the confusion, the sadness that had plagued her mortality. Believing what she learned would help others, she received heaven's permission to have me compile her story and then "give it to Sarah Hinze, who will know what to do with it." Susan thanked me and departed. I woke up with the conviction that Susan's message came by divine appointment. Her story must be told.

A few years before Susan died she confided to me that, as a child, she had recurring sensations of being born into the wrong family. Often she felt out of place, lonely, with no understanding as to why. Even her name seemed wrong. (To honor and protect my sister, I will not divulge her name. Susan is the name she believed she should have carried here.)

Susan described phobic childhood days when home alone while Mom worked. For reasons she could not explain, she feared no one would return for her. Her fears continued so strongly into adulthood that her health suffered, resulting in years of illness from which she often did not have the strength to overcome.

After years of suffering, Susan prayed more intently than ever for understanding regarding her emotional and physical afflictions. Within weeks of those prayers, there occurred two key events.

First, our father came to visit me. He confided a long withheld childhood memory. About age four, he was impressed that a little sister wanted to join the family. The feeling grew until he told his mother that a little sister would soon be born into their family. "I know she is coming," he concluded.

This was not welcome news to his worn down, discouraged mother.

She reprimanded his "silly idea." She had determined "never to bear another child."

Father's gaze was distant. "I don't know what happened to my sister. Perhaps it was childish imagination. But it seemed so real that I've never stopped wondering about her."

Witnessing the sincerity in my father's countenance, I, too, felt it was true—he should have had a younger sister.

A second piece of the puzzle came later that same week. Mother stopped by with another family secret, apparently unknown to Father. When Father was yet a small boy, his mother had, in fact, found herself pregnant against her desires. Before her pregnancy showed, and in keeping with her promise "never to bear another child," she made excuse to go into the city. Uncharacteristically, she insisted on traveling alone. She returned within days, no longer pregnant. Wherever she went during that week, Grandma had secretly aborted her child.

Shortly thereafter, I went to visit Susan, unaware of her recent prayers. Susan was attentive as I shared the stories from our divorced parents. She knew her prayers were being answered—she was the sister that her father had sensed at age four. She had tried to come, but her grandmother could not handle the burden. She, Susan, had been aborted and reassigned birth in the next generation.

Susan went into mourning. For weeks this middle-aged woman grieved for her own rejected little self of more than fifty years earlier, and for the grandmother who should have been her mother. She now understood her life long affinity for Grandma.

One day Susan asked me to take her to Grandma's grave. Frail though she was, she insisted on making her way alone to the site. In conversation, Susan was normally stoic, a listener, and a comfort to others. When I returned this day, she sobbed in ways I have never seen. Our roles reversed, I listened as she poured out sorrows pent up for decades.

These episodes endured about a year, near the end of which Susan reported a harrowing flashback, a pre-birth memory. She saw herself in heaven watching our grandmother having the abortion performed. Susan screamed, "Stop, stop! You have no idea what you are doing. Please stop, you can't do this!" Her intended mother did not hear. And she did not stop. In disbelief Susan watched her forming little body torn out, discarded.

Susan wrote her experience in a journal, providing insight into the feelings of the aborted ones. Key words included fear, abandonment, aloneness, grief, and most painful of all, rejection. Strangely there was also guilt. Somehow she felt responsible—if only she had been better. Next came jealousy; jealousy for others who had never been through this kind of trauma. And finally there was anger that she had to come a second time. She hated her true mother for having her killed, and for creating a lifetime of fear that it could happen again. Strong words, but that's what she wrote. It reminded me of something in the Bible about mothers who would kill their own daughters in the last days.

Susan suffered more than the rest of us. She once wrote of an exceptionally scary childhood day when she had been left alone. She watched a frightening movie, leading to terror that somebody was coming to force her into a big black coffin and carry her away into the sky. All her life she experienced such fears, along with a dread of rejection. She never felt she "belonged."

Susan believed that tendencies to do certain things, such as alcoholism or abortion, could be handed down from generation to generation. If negative tendencies are not eliminated from a family line, they can continue, and even get worse, causing pain and injury for generations. Learning the truth that she was aborted caused Susan much sorrow, but it also opened her spirit to the pain of her ancestors. For example, one day she was watching a television documentary on the Scottish people, our progenitors. Suddenly she felt the pain of abortion participants in her family line, both victims and perpetrators. Thus Susan's healing process included not only grief for her personal loss and for Grandma's loss, but also for all those in her family line afflicted by the tradition of abortion. She prayed that all might receive the balm of forgiveness.

Over time, Susan did forgive. Truth can be hard, but with it comes understanding. Truth became her ally. Susan released pain and fear and she forgave and healed emotionally. More, she healed   physically.

She enjoyed better health the last four years of her life than ever before. When it was her time to go, although the physical illness returned, the fear did not. There was contentment about her I'd never seen. It endured through her last breath. Truly she had overcome and returned to heaven in peace.

After Susan's death, a brother, who then knew nothing of what I have told, handed me a written account of his dream. Not many days after her passing, he saw Susan in heaven with our paternal grandmother. Puzzled but pleased, he said, "They were standing together, both radiant, and Susan and Grandma looked astonishingly alike—like sisters."

The circle was complete. Through the power of forgiveness Susan not only passed her greatest test, thus healing herself to return to heaven, but she also opened the way for Grandma to heal from the wrong she had done so they could be reunited as a family.

When writing this story, whisperings touched my soul, confirming that Susan's life-long wish to be reunited with her true mother was achieved. It was now so sweet.

I didn't cry much when Susan died. She suffered so on this earth that returning to heaven was surely a relief. But what comfort when my brother brought the news he'd seen her there with Grandma! At last I understand why Susan often lamented, "I just don't feel Grandma around. I can't feel her."
Well, now she does.

Rough Draft to Completed Manuscript

Writing a book with your spouse is a true test of love. We spent hours together each day; brainstorming, researching and writing. Night after night, we ate dinner while working at the computer and the momentum of the work kept us going, plus the fact that I give great back rubs.

I never knew Brent was such a gifted writer, but I wasn't surprised. We were on the Lord's errand. After a year, we were finished editing the third re-write of *The Castaways*.

Finally, the witness came. The book was complete.

After a few more proofreads, Brent and I decided to self-publish. This was something I had never considered doing before, but there was urgency with the message. The normal paths of publishing did not work with our timeline. In addition, we wanted to print the books economically enough that if necessary, we could give them away.

With the manuscript in hand, I drove it over to Laura's house. She was a new mother with her first son, Chandler and wanted to read what her father and I had been working on for a year.

Laura had always wanted to be a mother. She loved children and as a little girl wanted a dozen; six boys and six girls, but the traumatic pain she'd experienced during Chandler's birth left her uncertain if she would have another baby.

She had carried Chandler full-term when late one night her water broke. Together, Laura and her husband, Derek drove to the hospital, hopeful there son would soon be born. Hours went by, but Laura's labor didn't progress until she was given induction medication.

Labor did indeed start, but the side effects of the medication left her in terrible pain. Labor progressed faster then even the doctor realized. Pain medication was offered, but never took affect and after many excruciating hours of hard labor, Laura birthed a perfect 10-pound son.

I left the manuscript with Laura and was surprised when I heard from her the next morning. She was crying.

"Mom, all night I read *The Castaways*. I felt the love Jesus has for the babies. This book has helped me heal from my trauma of childbirth with Chandler."

Two years later, Laura gave birth to another child. Once again, her labor was difficult and pain medication didn't work, but her attitude was totally different. She was beaming.

"Mom, it's worth it," she said as she held another newborn son, Payson.

A Painting Comes Forth

When the idea to write *The Castaways* was given to me, I had an impression I needed a painting of Christ with a child or children on the cover. I had been looking at artwork and was impressed with an artist named David Lindsley. I called a publisher friend of mine who knew David and he told me he would have him contact me. Within 10 minutes, the phone rang and it was David on the other end. (Thank heavens none of my younger children were around to answer the phone that day.) I told David I loved his work and had a few of his art pieces in my home.

After describing my research I said, "I'm now writing a book about aborted children. For the cover I am impressed to find artwork of Christ with a child."

"I don't have anything that fits that idea, but may I paint one for you," he replied.

I couldn't believe it. David asked for a copy of *The Castaways* manuscript, which I immediately mailed to him. I waited to hear back and soon he sent me a sketch of his idea. It was perfect. Within several months, he had the painting completed.

David sent by mail an 8x12 imprint of *Safely in His Arms*. Brent and I were astonished that this beautiful rendition of Christ holding a child would honor *The Castaways*. The painting displayed Christ sitting near a golden curtain (representing the curtain that separates this world from heaven) holding an infant child in his lap. The painting conveyed the impression of great love and protection toward the child.

At last we had a beautiful cover and a completed manuscript. Brent and I found a small printing house in Salt Lake City that could print the book for an excellent price. We scheduled to print 5,000 copies when a friend of ours, a humanitarian who works internationally with children, asked if she could purchase 5,000 copies to distribute at United Nations conferences and to diplomats worldwide. The first printing was 10,000 copies and was scheduled to be released in September 2000.

I arranged a trip to Utah to speak to the Salt Lake City chapter of IANDS. The day I arrived the book was available, fresh off the press so to speak. I stopped by the printing house, picked up several boxes and carried them out to my car. I sat nearly breathless as I gently lifted a copy of *The Castaways* from the box and stared in reverie.

It's been said that an author looks at her new book the same way a mother looks at her new baby. There couldn't be a better analogy for how I felt at that moment. The idea had been conceived, labored and finally born. I drove across town on an emotional high. I had *The Castaways* and was moments from sharing its message with a large group of people.

I entered the room with a box of the new books in tow just minutes before the lecture was to start. I saw something that made me want to fall to me knees. High up on the wall of this beautiful conference room was David Lindsley's painting *Safely in His Arms*, the very one on my cover. It was massive, almost six feet tall. I couldn't take my eyes off it. There it was, in all its majesty. I had told David I was scheduled to speak in this building and to my surprise, he had brought the original painting and had it hung to greet me as I walked in the door.

I was already on cloud nine, but now I felt I could fly. I gave my lecture that night as I stood just underneath the image of Christ comforting the spirit of an aborted child. Later, a friend of mine in attendance told me that during my presentation she saw happy angel children of different races running up and down the aisles of the room.

Under a Full Moon

With the Lord's help and clever financing, we enjoyed our home in the desert with the pine and citrus trees. Our home had four bedrooms and four bathrooms, more than enough for a large family but with nine kids, we eventually converted the dining room, a two-car garage and an office into bedrooms. Seven bedrooms seemed to fit us better then four. Once again, Brent provided the outdoor entertainment with a trampoline, tree house, pool, jungle gym and tire swings. If a child wanted to flip, jump or propel, they found a way to do it.

One of the best things about an Arizona summer was swimming at night. When the sun finally set and the blaze of heat finally subsided, the children came alive. After dinner, they would quickly put on their bathing suits and run into the pool. Maybe other parents were tucking their children into bed, but at our house we swam night after night under a full moon. Because they were half Brent's, they were all excellent swimmers. I, on the other hand, didn't swim unless I had a floatie. I developed what I thought was a somewhat elegant stroke, but the kids called it a lame frog kick.

Brent and the kids would sometimes pull the trampoline up to the edge of the pool. The kids would bounce and flip into the water. I dodged them again and again. Eventually, I learned that when they were flipping and twirling, it was best to sit by the side of the pool with only my toes in the water.

Sharing the message of The Castaways

In late 2000, a girlfriend of mine who was involved in politics asked if I would go to Washington D.C with her. Once again I was sitting in a plane, clasping the handles of the seat, promising myself this was definitely my last cross-country flight ever. Surprisingly, she wasn't the only one who wanted me in Washington D.C. Months earlier, I had been asked by author Ned Dougherty (*Fast Lane to Heaven*) to come support him in a conference he was speaking at in Washington D.C. In addition, the National Right to Life March was taking place the same week. I felt compelled to go for many different reasons and as long as I was defending the unborn, I could do this.

The first morning in D.C, we planned a day of sightseeing. We decided to take the train from one historical sight to the other. Before we left the hotel, an impression came into my mind to put several copies of *The Castaways* into my purse. For a moment I paused. The last thing I wanted to do was carry around a purse full of books, but I knew better then to ignore the reassuring voice in my mind.

Later that day, while standing in the Capital Rotunda, looking at the original document of the U.S. Constitution, the voice from earlier came into my mind again.

"See that lady standing on the other side of the room? You are to give her a copy of *The Castaways*."

I knew the voice well and the awkwardness of going up to a total stranger would not stop me. Like an obedient child, I started my walk across the room.

I introduced myself and handed her a copy of my book.

"You are Sarah Hinze?" the lady said in a thick French accent.

She seemed to know me.

I nodded my head, wondering if we had met before.

"Sarah, I have all your books. They mean the world to me. Your books make me feel closer to heaven. I didn't know you had a new book out?"

"Thank you so much. Yes, this new book shares the message of aborted children. I call them the castaways."

She asked if I would sign her book, which I did, adding my phone number and website as well. She thanked me and left.

Ten years later the phone rang and I heard a familiar voice with a French accent. I immediately knew it was the same woman.

"I've been following your writings and have purchased many of your books throughout the years, giving them away to friends and family as gifts. I need to tell you what has happened. About six months ago, a neighbor of mine came over and told me her teenage daughter was pregnant and planning an abortion. Sarah, I knew just what to do. I went to my bookshelf and handed her a copy of *The Castaways*. A few days later, the neighbor came back to tell me, 'There's something special about that little book you gave me. My daughter read it and has decided to save the child. She's not having an abortion.'

"Sarah, we were all thrilled. Today she had the little baby, a boy, and she gave him up for adoption. You saved the life of that child. You need to know that."

I reflected back ten years earlier, filling my purse with books that I knew would be heavy to carry throughout the day and never would I have imagined by obeying that inner voice, I would ten years later hear about a child whose life had been spared.

A Special Visitor

I suppose by now it comes as no surprise that the unborn hosts of heaven are at times very near to me. Sometimes just before I give a talk, I am almost overcome with their energy as they fill the room. Their energy is of a high vibration and as it mingles with my spirit, I am brought to tears and I struggle to contain my composure. It is because of the great love that they bring with them. They are love. They have unconditional love for their families, their parents, and their brothers and sisters.

Some who have attended my talks have felt or seen their own unborn, miscarried or aborted children sitting or standing next to them, sometimes even holding their hands.

Others have seen someone standing with me when I speak. Brent and I were asked to speak on *The Castaways* in San Antonio at a Christian Family Conference.

The location of the lecture was a resort-style ranch in the country, with a hotel and a dozens of luxury cabins for guests.

Brent and I were staying in a cabin and I spent the morning reading through my notes. Although I take notes with me up to the podium, I usually do not read my talk. I like to look into the eyes of the audience as I speak.

"Ready?" Brent asked, his notes in a file tucked underneath his arm. "It's time to go."

We walked through the beautiful forest of the resort and made our way into a large assembly room, filled with over 200 chairs. People were gathering into their seats and Brent and I were escorted to two chairs on the corner of the stage. Before we were introduced, a harpist played a short piece she had composed. The perfection of hearing heavenly music from a harpist as I prepared to speak left me with a humble feeling. The tone was set. Brent and I were introduced and I stood up to speak.

I shared my message of the angel children like I had many times before. When Brent and I finished speaking, some from the audience gathered around us to share their thoughts. After I finished visiting with a few interested audience members, an older lady I had noticed while I was speaking, motioned for me to come with her off stage.

I followed her to the back of the room.

"Sarah, my name is Ruth. Your message was very touching, but more than that, during your talk there was suddenly a beautiful woman standing next to you. She was a woman of light and had the beauty of an ancient queen.

Ruth was a spiritual soul, maybe in her early 80s, with great love shining from her aged face. Hers was a face without guile.

I thought of my friend, Dr. Elisabeth Kübler-Ross, who often referred to angels in her work. Elisabeth felt there were special ministering angels on behalf of children and children who had died. On occasion some people over the years had seen them at Elisabeth's lectures. I had seen the many statues and paintings of angels on my occasional visits to Elisabeth's home in Scottsdale, Arizona.

In one of these tender visits, Elisabeth told me, "The day will come when someone gifted with spiritual vision will see angels involvement with your mission. It is a holy work that you are involved in."

Thinking of Elisabeth's counsel caused me to somewhat gain my composure.

I was suddenly focusing again on this kind woman as she looked directly into my soul.

"No, Ruth, I did not see what you saw, but I believe you did."

Ruth and I hugged once more and she departed, leaving me alone near the back of the room. I looked up at Brent who was still visiting with members of the audience, my love for him surged to new heights. Was this really happening? Was a message as simple as we come from and return to heaven really touching people's lives?

What Happens to a Mother Who Aborts Her Child?

Up until this point in my research, my main concern had been the physical, emotional and spiritual pain of aborted babies. Now I was beginning to understand the pain of mothers who had lost their babies to abortion. As a researcher, I attended pro-life meetings. I wanted to learn from a grassroots level what was being said, perceived and the energy of how they were accomplishing what they wanted to do. What were they teaching? What were their goals?

I was impressed with much of it, but the anger and hostility of some of the individuals directed toward woman who had abortions left me uncomfortable. I did not feel the Lord felt this way towards women who had abortions. If anything, the Lord wanted them to heal. No good comes out of darkness and Christ stands ready to comfort all who suffer from abortion trauma. In addition, based on an experience several years earlier, I knew at least some aborted ones—the victims— forgave and still loved their mothers who had rejected them by abortion:

After speaking to a group of people at a bookstore in Phoenix, I made my way to the back of the room and introduced myself to a couple who appeared quite emotional during my presentation. The young woman, teary-eyed, told their story. "We have never attended a lecture like this, but when we saw the posters on your topic we were compelled to come. While your friend sang that beautiful opening song about children, I felt a child's hand take mine. Instantly I knew it was the daughter we had aborted two years ago, before we married. She stayed with us throughout your presentation. I never imagined an aborted child still existed. Could she still want us after what we did to her?"

I offered what comfort I could, encouraging them to take that leap of faith and invite their daughter to come again. As they departed with hope in their hearts, I marveled at the power of eternal bonds. Even after the pain of abortion, some of heaven's pure and innocent children have so perfected their capacity for love that they willingly forgive, return to, and love the very parents who rejected them.

Who forgives and loves those who take their life? Many castaways may be suffering, but they also have a remarkable capacity to love. *The Castaways* was not only a book of understanding and warning to those considering abortion, but a book of hope to those who'd already made their choice.

Another life saved

Brent and I had just returned from speaking at another conference and were greeted by our nine children, eager to be reunited with their parents. We were getting reacquainted with the hustle and bustle of our busy home when the phone rang. One of the conference directors was on the other end of the phone.

"Sarah, I'm so glad I've caught you. We have an emergency on our hands at my house and you're the only person I could think to call."

I sat and listened intently.

"I just learned my daughter has scheduled to have an abortion. She had no intention of telling me, but I saw it written on her calendar. I've tried everything to talk her out of it and she won't listen. Sarah, can you please talk to her."

With a prayer in my heart I said, "Yes, please put her on the phone."

What could I say? Your unborn child lives in heaven and is

awaiting his or her birth? Your child has an important mission to fulfill on earth? Would she believe me? The idea came into my mind to share a story I had collected years earlier. I opened *The Castaways* and with a little explanation, started reading the following:

My precious son,

I do not know how you feel toward me . . . At the time I became pregnant with you . . . I had just turned seventeen.

Eventually, with the . . . help of a [minister], I told my parents of the pregnancy, and we proceeded with making plans on what to do. After much counsel and prayer . . . I made the decision to have you and give you up for adoption. . .

My parents felt I should live with a foster family in another state until after the birth and arrangements were made. I now understand the wisdom of their decision, but at the time, I was angry and felt as if I was being "put away" to hide their shame. I did not want to go, and as the time for me to leave drew near, I became desperate to find a way to stay home.

I had always been strongly opposed to abortion, but with these difficult pressures I found myself thinking about it occasionally, and even considering it. If I could just remove the presence of the baby, I could move on with my life and everything could go on as it had been. No more problems. No fears. No shame. No facing up to my mistake.

The idea of having an abortion actually started to sound like my solution. I really did not want an abortion, but I was feeling desperate. I knew I had to act quickly as my flight was scheduled to leave within a few days. Each clinic I called was unable to fit me into their schedule until well after my flight out of state.

I was emotionally exhausted when I finally hung up the phone. I went into my room, turned off the light, and crawled into bed, where I cried myself to sleep . . . I can still remember the dream I had as clearly as if it were yesterday.

In my dream, it was a few weeks before your scheduled delivery date, and I was lying on a table in the doctor's office having an examination. The doctor wanted to make sure that you were growing properly and wanted to take your weight and measurements. He made an incision in my abdomen and carefully removed you from my womb. I watched as he had you weighed and measured. Everything was just fine, and you were developing normally into a fine, healthy baby. I was enjoying the experience, yet at the same time I was still searching for a way in which I would not have to follow through with the whole ordeal. For a moment, I considered telling the doctor not to put you back into my womb: to stitch me up and just let me walk away.

But at that moment, a wonderful thing happened. You suddenly turned your head and reached out for me, your big eyes glistening with tears. I could not resist the urge to pick you up. As I held you close, you wrapped your tiny arms around my neck with the strength of an adult and would not let me put you down. I could feel your desperation to cling to life, and I knew then that it was a small sacrifice for me to provide that life for you. The doctor and his office slowly faded away, and you and I were left alone, still clinging to each other.

When I awoke the next morning, I told my mother about the dream. . . that now I knew without a doubt that my child had a right to live, a right to be born into this world and experience the joys, as well as the sorrows, that this life can bring. My sweet son, please believe me when I say how much I love you!

I thought over every possible solution concerning my keeping and raising you. . . . I prayed to keep you, but never felt [right] about it . . . I know I made the right decision in having you adopted, but it is the hardest thing I have ever done. You were such a beautiful baby, and I loved you so much.

I felt that another couple that was prepared to start a family but could have none of their own would be able to provide for you far more adequately than I. With me your life would start in shame, guilt, and sorrow, and without a father to love you as your adoptive father now loves you.

I truly believe that we are, in some way, assigned children in our pre-earth existence. At one point as I deliberated, I wondered if I might be giving up one of my assigned children by placing you up for adoption. But before I reached a conclusion, I had another thought. What happens to the children assigned to a couple who are physically unable to have any of their own? The moment I had that question, it was answered in my mind. The couples adopt them. Each time the child seems to fit so perfectly into the family. I then realized that I was actually carrying a child that had been assigned to another couple. I hope you understand. Even though I am the person who carried you and gave you birth, your mom and dad are actually your true parents.

Though all my wishes are that I could watch you grow up to be a handsome young man, I know deep in my heart that I have done the right thing. I hope someday in the eternities we may meet and share our feelings face to face. I love you son, and always will.

Forever my love, Mom

After reading the letter I said, "I believe this unborn child was allowed to appear to his biological mother in a dream so he could help her heart to change. The teen mother's heart was touched, strengthening her love and courage to proceed with the pregnancy. When her son was born, the young mother had peace of mind in giving her son to a childless couple whom she believed had been assigned to adopt, love and raise the boy. This solution was an answer to prayer for the unwed mother, the baby, and the childless couple who were eager to begin a family."

I paused. I could hear the girl on the other end of the phone crying quietly. Very softly I asked, "What are you feeling?"

"So many of my friends have had abortions, but I can't do it. I don't know what I was thinking."

The grateful mother called me back a few days later and shared the good news that her daughter had decided to keep the baby and place him for adoption to a good family.

Six months later, the mother called again with an update. The baby was born and her daughter had picked the adoptive parents. The young woman was grateful to know the baby was with such a good family.

Experiences like this were very rewarding to us, but, like everyone else, we were juggling family, work, and many other things all at the same time. Then a family crisis struck when my mother in Tennessee had a serious stroke. Brent and I arranged to go back to visit her and see what we should do to help her during this ordeal.

My Parents Together Forever

After Dad died, Mom managed well for several years. She missed Dad terribly, but dealt with the loneliness by caring for relatives and neighbors in need. Still, her daily prayers included the same request: "I'm ready. Please take me home to Lawrence."

One night she awoke to see Dad standing in the bedroom doorway. He expressed his love to her and described the home he was building for them in heaven where they would be together again. Ironically, there had been a time when my mom had been the one preparing a home for him while he was away at war.

A year after my parents were married, my father served in England as a medic during World War II. Mom had saved her money and bought a little house so when he came home they would be ready to start their family. She told me about the night he came home. He had taken the train into town and caught a ride to her mom's house. He stood on the front porch late at night, knocking on the door. She ran to open it, but for the life of her, she couldn't figure out how to unlock the deadbolt. They stood staring each other through the glass, smiling from ear to ear while my grandmother struggled to open the door. What a treasured thought to think that in the spirit world Dad was preparing a home for Mom when she crossed over to the other side.

After Mom's stroke, we arranged to bring this lifelong Tennessee girl to live with us in the Arizona desert. She said good-bye to the canopy of poplar trees lining her neighborhood streets and moved to find 10-foot saguaro cacti everywhere.

For several months Mom's health improved. She grew closer to her grandchildren and great-grand children than ever before. She swam with them in the pool and took short walks with them up and down the cul-de-sac. She still prayed daily to go to heaven and be with Lawrence. Then Alzheimer's set in with all of its complications. In a few months more, Mom refused to eat, became weak and eventually comatose, and had to be moved to a hospice center.

The day before she died I was sitting by her bed when I sensed my father's presence. He stood by the sliding glass door that opened onto the patio.

We communicated mind to mind. He thanked our family for taking such good care of Mom and was excited about their future in the home he had prepared for her in heaven. Just before he left, I asked if he would come for Mom when it was her time. He promised me, "You'll know I came for her, because when she sees me she will die with a smile on her face."

I sat with Mom through the night. Early in the morning I left for home to get my younger children off to school. I was about to go back to the hospice when the phone rang—Mom had just passed away.

Strangely, at first I felt little sorrow, only happiness that my parents were again together. In ten minutes I arrived back at the hospice center, parked the van and rushed to Mom's room in anticipation. Sure enough, her frail face, which had been expressionless in her coma, was bathed in a contented smile.

I sensed Mom and Dad's presence by the patio doors. They had waited for me to share in their joy. Mom whispered to my mind, "Your dad is so handsome! And I am young and beautiful again, wearing his favorite; a full skirt with a slender waist. I am so happy."

Then from Dad I heard, "There is a conduit of light by the patio door through which I will take your mother to our home. Loved ones and friends are waiting there in celebration. We want you to speak at the funeral to honor your mother."

Brent and I flew back to Tennessee to start on funeral preparations. Later at my aunt's house, I had second thoughts about the program. I knew Mom could not be honored properly without Dad. She was too much a part of him to have it any other way. I called the funeral home, hoping there was still time to make changes.

They hadn't printed the program yet and were open to my requests. I said, "Instead of just Mom's picture on the program, please use the picture of both Mom and Dad, and underneath write the words, 'Together Forever.'"

That's better. I thought to myself.

I know that death is not the end. Life continues in another dimension, more vibrant and meaningful then anything we've experienced of earth. In heaven we are free of pain, sorrow, illness and disappointment. We are with family and friends we love. Relationships, character and knowledge are the only things we can take with us when we die. We will remember our previous life in heaven with God and Jesus before we were born. Our earth life with all its tests and trials will make sense. Our great quest before we were born was to come to earth and gain knowledge by what we experience.

I missed my mother, but knew of the great reunion she and Dad were sharing.

The evening I spoke at her funeral, I could feel my parents next to me during part of my talk. Their presence felt like a light inside me. Later, my mom's best friend, Beryl, told me when I began to speak, she saw my mother's face shine through me. Then toward the end of the talk she saw my father's face. That was very comforting to me.

Early the next morning, we drove through the scenic country side of the Smokey Mountains to the cemetery where we'd laid Dad to rest eight years earlier. Sunshine sparkled through air washed clean by rain during the night. We followed pallbearers and casket across damp grass to the gravesite. I paused reverently before the weathered headstone and read the words engraved beneath their names—"Together Forever."

They had prepared the stone with those words long before either of them died. I had forgotten, but they did not.

It is my humble belief that when we die, someone, or many, will come for us. No one ever dies alone. We have a destiny beyond this life.

And heaven is where dreams come true.

Am I a Child of God?

I received a phone call from a gentleman named Tony from New York City. He had read *Coming from the Light* and called with one question: "Is it true—is it really true? Am I really a child of God?"

"Yes," I assured him.

Tony was suffering from a terminal illness. We talked about many things—his upbringing in a very abusive home—from his mother. He had never emotionally recovered from all that she had put him through. He cried as he told me about events in his life. Because of his abuse, he had never married and never had children. He regretted that fact, now that his time on earth was almost over. Tony lived longer than expected and called me every few months for several years. I always enjoyed his calls. I prayed for him over the phone and encouraged him to find Jesus. It has been years since I've heard from him and I think he has passed to the otherside. If so, he now knows for certain he is a child of God.

Angels Assigned to Help the Castaways

A woman who had read *The Castaways* called and described a comforting experience while attending her friend's funeral. After a year of fighting cancer, with many highs and lows and many hopes that she would survive, this woman's friend suddenly died.

"She had four young children so I wondered, why would God take a young mother back to heaven when she had such purpose here on earth?"

"While listening to the words of the closing song at the funeral, a vision of my friend came into my mind. I saw her in heaven holding a baby. She had a smile on her face and was peacefully rocking the baby in a rocking chair. The vision wasn't far-fetched at all. My friend had always loved babies and whenever possible would hold the newborn of friends and family. She was well-known as a baby lover and would have had more of her own, but health reasons prevented it. Suddenly it all became clear to me—my friend was in heaven caring for the babies and those who had been castaway."

A New Easter Dress from my Mother

About nine months after the death of my mom, I had a wonderful dream about her. I was with my children in the dream and they were all much younger. Some of the children were babies in the dream but they talked to me as adults.

I came to a two-story home that was very tidy around the outside with beautiful flowers growing in a variety of colors. I took the children inside and they began to run around and play. From the staircase, I noticed a beautiful light began to form, and the light began to move down the stairs.

As I adjusted my eyes to the light, my mother came into focus. She was radiant, dressed in a beautiful pink suit, with a straight skirt and a short sleeve jacket, like an Easter Sunday suit that women wore in her days as a young mother. She looked beautiful, slim, and so happy. I ran to her and called to the children, "It's Grandma Street."

We were all happy and ran to her. I was overcome with emotion and could only say, "Mama, Mama."

That was all I could say. I held her. She was real. I could embrace her. I thought that I was in her home that dad had built for her in heaven. It looked like her home that she had as a young woman, only prettier, but the same floor plan. When I woke up, I could feel my mother with me in my room. It was a tender time and I knew that she had visited me to let me know that she was happy.

Traditionally, Easter is one of my family's favorite times. We plan a big dinner on Easter Sunday and after dinner have an Easter egg hunt in our acre yard with the citrus trees still hanging full of oranges and grapefruit. It was one of my mom's favorite times when she lived with us. She took great delight with the little grandchildren, the toddlers and those who were still full of wonder for the Easter bunny. We felt it a sacred time as we watched the little ones go around the yard with their older siblings helping them, laughing and playing.

It was the day before Easter Sunday and I was running errands in the afternoon to finish up the final plans. While driving by one of the many strip malls in our town, I suddenly had a very unusual thought, "If you will pull over and go into a certain department store, you will find on the shelves the same dress and jacket in your size that your mother was wearing in your dream last night."

That thought was intriguing enough that I was willing to check it out. I pulled into the parking lot and walked into the store. I walked back to the women's dresses in my size and began to sort through them to see if there was anything in pink. Finally I came to some pink fabric on the hangers.

"Surely, this can't be for real," I thought, but there it was—a full dress with a pink skirt and a pink jacket with short sleeves, just like the one in my dream that mom was wearing. The style was not of the 1950s but of current fashion, yet it was unmistakably the same dress.

My mom, who always bought my sister Sandra and I a new Easter dress every year when we were children, was picking out an Easter dress for me this year. I would not have bought one for myself, but since my mom had picked this one out, I took it to the check out and bought it.

My mother had directed me to an Easter dress she had picked out for me from the other side. She still wanted me to know I was her little girl.

Children Playing in the Trees

One of my most remarkable experiences with the angel children occurred at an event in Ciudad Juarez, Mexico. Our group was staying at the home of a lovely older couple. One morning our hostess went next door to visit her friend. When she returned she told me that her friend had had a restless night in which she had a dream and saw many children in her home who were sad and trying to get everyone's attention.

Immediately I knew these children were castaways. My hostess picked up a copy of *The Castaways* that was sitting on the kitchen table, looked at the cover and commented, "Oh my goodness. So this little book is true." I smiled and nodded in agreement.

The following afternoon my dear friends, Elane Durham, a near-death survivor and author, artist David Lindsley, and I were honored at a reception in an older home in the city which had been converted into a bookstore. Outside the home there was a stately courtyard and an expansive backyard with large trees standing as sentinels.

The spirit of love and interest in our information and materials was very strong as many people filed in and greeted us. One woman grabbed me and surprised me with a big, enthusiastic hug. As I looked into her face, I was overcome with the love of God that shone on her countenance.

After visiting with her for awhile, I walked outside into the courtyard. It was a beautiful warm day with not even a wisp of wind. Strangely, the huge trees in the back were swaying too and fro, bending deeply at each sway. I wondered, "What in the world is going on with those trees? How can they bend like that when there is not so much as a breeze?"

Suddenly my spiritual eyes were opened and I saw them—the trees were full of children! They were joyfully playing and swinging in the tree tops. It was as if their joy was contagious and the very trees had joined the children in their exuberance, so happy they were to have them there. These enthusiastic children were of all ages, boys and girls all dressed in white. Even though I sensed that some were castaways, all had joy on their faces. Why? In reply, this message entered my mind, "The unborn children are joyous that their future parents and loved ones will read stories of *The Castaways* and their hearts will be changed toward them."

I was blown away. Could it really be that this mission I feared was impossible in our day and age—this mission of changing hearts toward the unborn—was actually happening? I was doing my small part, but heaven was doing the rest. I gazed back up at the children—so happy, so hopeful that their turn on earth was coming. Tears blurred my vision. I blinked . . . and they were gone. And the trees ceased to sway.

That evening I spoke in the quaint old bookstore. I asked the woman to whom I had been so drawn to earlier in the day if she would be my translator. Graciously, she agreed. She had also mentioned that during the day, she had already read most of *The Castaways*.

After speaking for a short while—first my words in English, then a pause while she expressed my message in Spanish—the process was slow and a bit tedious. Interestingly, the spirit was so strong with her that I was impressed to ask her to finish my talk in Spanish. She did. I did not understand her words but I knew she said what the Lord wanted to be spoken.

I thought of the words of C.S. Lewis:

It is a serious thing to remember that any person you talk to may one day be a creature which, if you saw it now, you would be strongly tempted to worship. There are no ordinary people. You have never talked to a mere mortal. Next to God himself, your neighbor is the holiest object presented to your senses.

Meeting Dr. Elisabeth Kübler-Ross

Dr. Elisabeth Kübler-Ross moved from Switzerland to America and became a pioneer in near-death studies and the establishment of hospice in the United States and throughout the world. Her lectures and books, including the best seller, *On Death and Dying*, have brought comfort and healing to countless thousands of individuals in the grieving and dying process.

Although retired and suffering the after-effects of a stroke, in the mid-1990s Dr. Kübler-Ross granted Brent and I several visits in her Arizona home. We drove north of Scottsdale, seemingly past civilization. Soon we turned off the pavement onto desert trails. The directions she had given us were very Native American, such as—"go left at the tall saguaro cactus, right in two tenths of a mile at the Palo Verde tree, left again at the blackened stump charred by lightning during a monsoon storm . . ."

After ten minutes of striving to follow the directions and not a home in sight, we were beginning to feel lost. Suddenly we burst out laughing, for there in this desert wilderness appeared a lone street sign labeled: Elisabeth.

We followed the arrow and soon pulled up in front of Elisabeth's pretty Mexican style adobe home with teepee and totem pole out front. Looking off through the desert bordered by distant purple mountains, it was very clear—Elisabeth loved solitude.

A caregiver rushed out in warm greeting and invited us indoors where we wound around through a lifetime of mementos from all over the world. On the far end of the room sat Elisabeth in her wheelchair. In her seventies, the stroke she had suffered left one side of her body mostly paralyzed. With a kind smile, she extended her good hand to welcome us. She was more diminutive in body than we had expected, but mighty in conversation and wit. She had sculptures and paintings of the Virgin Mary displayed around her desert cabin.

For about two hours this frail woman graciously answered our questions about her exceptional career with a charming sense of humor, and in return displayed keen interest in our prebirth research.

She asked me to go in the kitchen and make her a pastrami sandwich. "The pastrami is just in the refrigerator, she said. Put pickles on it, and lots of mustard. Just make me a sandwich and Brent and I will write up your endorsement."

I stood in front of a very large stainless steel refrigerator. When I opened it, I gasped. Food filled every shelf up to the top. Stacks and stacks of everything imaginable. I said a little prayer, "Lord, where is the pastrami?"

I mustered all of my faith and reached into one of the shelves. My hand landed on a white package and I picked it up. Upon opening it, to my surprise, it was pastrami!

Pickles and mustard were searched out too. Finally the sandwich was made and it was spectacular!

I brought it to Elisabeth and she announced, "We have written your endorsement. I hope that you like it."

She read it to me:

"For years I have taught that we come from the same Source at birth and we return to the Source at death. The Source is God, who has many names. Earth experience is for our growth and spiritual development. When we

*have learned and taught what we came to earth for, we graduate—death
is graduation.*

*"We have learned much about life after death. Sarah Hinze leads us into
the next great area of research—the study of where we come from."*

I went back several times to visit Elisabeth, either alone or with
other friends. We had several talks during that time that were most
endearing.

Brent and I attended her funeral. Dignitaries were there from all
over the world to honor her for the contributions she had made in the
area of care and understanding of the dying and bereaved. Her work
changed the way the terminally ill are treated. She had been nominated
for a Nobel Peace Prize and had received worldwide honors. Now she
was free of her tired and broken body—dancing among the stars as she
had wanted for a long time.

Had I Done as the Lord Wanted?

One night I lay in bed wondering, "Have my books made a difference
in the world?" I fell asleep and had a dream in which my father was taking
me to home after home after home, showing me children playing with
toys, babies being held by their mothers, a daddy swinging a little girl in
his arms.

Dad said to me, "These are some of the homes where your books have
touched hearts. When you pass over to the other side, then you will see
the full picture. Your books have made a difference."

I awakened smiling. I felt content. I thought about the love I've had
with my own children. The treasures in my life are in the eyes of my
family, my husband, children and grandchildren.

I remembered an experience I'd had when *Coming from the Light*
first came out. Simon & Schuster sent me on a book tour. Following a
short stay in New York City, I visited Canada and then Chicago. Laura was
20 years old and volunteered to babysit for the week I was gone. When I
flew back to Arizona, Brent picked me up at the airport and I couldn't wait
to get home.

When we arrived at our home, I ran into the house very emotional. I
was home with my family again! Laura was playing tea party with her baby

sisters, Rachel and Anna. The girls were caught up in play when Anna turned toward me. "Here, Mommy, this is your cup," I sat down on the floor next to her. Rachel handed me a little plate with a sandwich on it. "We missed you, Mommy," she said. They had their baby dolls in their laps and were pretending to give them sips of water.

I paused in the moment, marveling that these little princesses were the same girls who had come to me from heaven years earlier, asking to be my daughters. I remembered clearly their beautiful adult features of their faces. Now, here they were with their little chubby cheeks and vivid imaginations, playing like they, too, were mommies.

I will always marvel at the joy a little girl has playing with a doll. It's like they instinctively know they were born to be mothers. Later, both girls sat on my lap while I told them about the places I'd been and the people I'd seen. They cuddled into me and I could almost smell the sunshine in their hair.

I was happy to be home with my greatest treasure, my family. Being a wife and mother is the most heartwarming and rewarding thing I have done with my life. I hoped then and still do, that I can convey this same love of self, family and God to others.

To be continued . . .

I'm rushing to get my son Sam off to school and considering he's a senior in high school, I'm not in the best mood.

"Did you finish your homework?" I ask, making sure to add a hint of annoyance in my voice.

He's going to be late. His two younger sisters left for school more than ten minutes ago.

"I finished around midnight, and thanks for breakfast," he says, giving me a kiss on my cheek.

I can't stay mad at this kid for long. The phone rings and I hug Sam just as he runs out the door.

Sam is the last boy at home. His older brothers are already out on their own, either in college or married.

"Hello," I say on the other end of the line, wondering if it is my oldest daughter, Krista. She's expecting a baby any day now.

"Hi," an unfamiliar female voice says. "I'm calling to speak with Sarah Hinze."

"This is Sarah. How can I help you?"

"You don't know me and I hope I'm not disturbing you," the woman says. "It's just—I just finished your book. I'm not sure what I'm thinking to be calling you like this, but I had an experience several years ago that I've never shared with anyone. After reading your book, I think I need to talk about it."

I ask her name, then grab my pen and notepad. I wait as she emotionally prepares herself to share with me her memory.

I am standing, all giggly, in front of the Pocket Books Emblem at the Simon & Schuster Building in New York City, with my new book Coming from the Light. I had taken a very early flight there from Washington, D.C. and had gone 48 hours without sleep.

All of our children, taken 1993. Laura, Rod, Tadd, Matthew, Krista, Becky, Rachel, Brent, Sarah (holding Anna), and Sam.

Family Photo of our adult children taken 2008. Becky, Rod, Tadd, Krista, Matthew, Sam, Laura, Anna, Sarah, Brent, and Rachel.

Brent and I in 2008 among the orange trees at our home in Arizona.

Our Thanksgiving family photo in 2009 with all of our adult children and their families, including Brent's sister Aunt Vickie Hinze.

Our annual Easter celebration under the giant pines of our Arizona home.

AFTERWORD

by Laura Hinze Lofgreen

For months, my mom and I worked on stories for *The Memory Catcher*. She pulled out boxes of journals, old photographs and newspaper clippings. I marveled at her ideas, read through old manuscripts and was wowed by her accomplishments, including author of six books. While my mom and I laughed about old memories and cried about loved ones now gone back to heaven, my dad turned the computer on in the other room and started writing.

Eventually, my dad came to us with what he wrote. It was good, and it's no surprise, he knows my mom better then anyone. Such was the start of *The Memory Catcher*. With all the information my mom and I had, I'm not sure where we would have begun. Plus, with all the fun we were having, really, who had time to write! So thank you, Dad, for getting us launched!

My mom has always said we were made out of the same stardust. As a girl, I envisioned God sprinkling her and me with the same sweet pixie dust while we giggled with joy that we were to be mother and daughter. We have the same blonde hair, the same nose, the same laugh, but it's more then our physical similarities.

Our lives together have revolved around the same themes. When I'm sad, so is she. When I want a dog, she's just found one looking for a good home. When she wants to go on an adventure, I've already pulled in the driveway wondering if she wants to spend the day with me and my kids (trust me, that is an adventure for sure). In so many ways, we complete each other and there's an innocence that comes from loving someone that much. She laughs at my jokes just as I point out that she really is funny, even when she doesn't know it. I have loved my mom forever.

My mom is never stingy with compliments. As a young girl, I knew my mom thought I was special. The first time I cooked, she said it was the best thing she'd every eaten. She not only praised me for my accomplishments, but she noticed when I was kind and good to others. She called me a peacemaker and said I was Christ- like. I feel these attributes she sees in me are what make her the proudest.

Every day, before we started working on *The Memory Catcher*, my mom and I had prayer. I shouldn't have been surprised by her heartfelt gratitude expressed to God that we had the opportunity to write together, but I was. She didn't just thank Him; she poured her heart out to Him. My entire life I've prayed with my mom, but these prayers were different. She prayed with a maturity and a desire that let me know what was expected of us. Writing her biography was a big task and we couldn't do it without His help. In addition, she prayed reverently for me and my family, that I would be blessed for my efforts. I was humbled to have someone pray for me with such intensity.

Several weeks into the writing, I began to understand more and more how the Lord works in my mom's life. She lives by the charge to "always have a prayer in your heart." God is constantly at the forefront of her thoughts. Every spiritual experience she shared seemed to point to the same truth; that God not only loves us, but He always wants to be with us. He clearly had something for her to accomplish and I was beginning to understand just how literally she took His assignment.

Then, my mom shared with me her experience where in a spiritual experience she saw the earth from a great distance. She saw that the earth is covered with spiritual darkness, and then she and her escort stopped above China with its "one child policy." Listening to the cries of the castaways in this experience (and others) has unmistakably been one of the most painful experiences of her life. I had heard this story before, but this time I was in tears. Where before it seemed this was just her idea, I now knew it really happened—where before I was a supporter, now I was a believer.

And now it was I who was wondering what God wanted me to do. My task to help Mom write became a quest to capture my own mission as well as understand who my mom truly is. Day after day, I was honored to be with this woman who was sharing her soul through real-life stories and inspiration. Stories I'd heard my entire life took on new meaning. She understood things of eternity I would never know. I knew what God had asked her to do and believed in her mission wholeheartedly. Her assignment was heavy and at times I wondered if she felt overwhelmed. Still, she knew what she had to do and she was doing it beautifully. A warm spirit entered my heart. Although she was mortal I kind of saw her as an angel on the Lord's mission.

That evening I got my kids ready for bed. I tucked my 4 year- old son under his covers, anxious to get back to writing when he requested I cuddle with him. I climbed into his bed and took him into my arms, smelling his just shampooed hair. My mind pondered God's love for children as I thought about the stories of *The Memory Catcher*.

"Mommy, I love you," Reef interjected. I was stirred at the love I felt from and toward this child. For weeks I had been so preoccupied with writing, but here he was, my perfect little child who I had always wanted. It was such a pleasure to be his mother, to see him day after day grow and be happy and eat healthy food. My heart seemed to soar with gratitude that I was a mother...his mother. I have five beautiful children and now understand better through my mom the privilege it is to have them given to me by God.

I kissed Reef on his head. "I love you too," I replied, while contemplating my own mother. How she loved me and my siblings! How she loved being a mother! She would do anything for us. Yes, to me she is an angel.

With that thought I flashed back to Mom—her beauty and her heavenly smile. I had been with an angel, not just writing this book, but for my entire life. Anyone who puts the Lord first in their life, who shares their talents with others, who listens with their heart as well as their mind, who makes noble sacrifices for others and who wants desperately to do the will of Jesus, is an angel.

May we all recognize the angels in our own life and care for and love one another as God would have us do.

CONTACT INFORMATION FOR SARAH HINZE

Please contact us with any questions or additional stories you may have to add to our research, to purchase additional books, or to speak to your group at:

www.sarahhinze.com or **sarah@sarahhinze.com**

www.rememberingheavenmovie.com

sarahhinze.hinze@gmail.com

All of our books are on Amazon and can be viewed and purchased at www.sarahhinze.com/home/books2/

ABOUT THE AUTHORS

Sarah Hinze is the memory catcher. She and her husband Brent reside in Arizona and are the parents of 9 children and 21 grandchildren, so far. She is the author of *Life Before Life, Coming from the Light, We Lived in Heaven, The Castaways,* and *Songs of the Morning Stars.* She blogs at www.sarahhinze.com

Laura Hinze Lofgreen is married to the love of her life, Derek. Together they have five children—four boys and one precious girl, all named after Arizona towns. She blogs at www.mydeartrash.com.
The Memory Catcher is her first book.

Sitting with Laura's daughter (my granddaughter) Eden Garland.

www.ingramcontent.com/pod-product-compliance
Lightning Source LLC
Chambersburg PA
CBHW060244050426
42448CB00009B/1575